ARMY
BRAT

Also by William Jay Smith

POETRY

Poems • Celebration at Dark • Poems
1947—1957 • The Tin Can and Other
Poems • New & Selected Poems • Venice
in the Fog • Journey to the Dead Sea • The
Traveler's Tree, New and Selected Poems •
(FOR CHILDREN) Laughing Time • Boy
Blue's Book of Beasts • Puptents and
Pebbles • Typewriter Town • What Did I
See? • Big and Little: *Little Dimity, Big
Gumbo, Big and Little* • Ho for a Hat! • If I
Had a Boat • Mr. Smith and Other
Nonsense • Laughing Time, Nonsense
Poems

TRANSLATIONS

Poems of a Multimillionaire,
by Valery Larbaud • Selected Writings of
Jules Laforgue • Two Plays by Charles
Bertin: *Christopher Columbus* and *Don Juan* •
(FOR CHILDREN) The Children of the Forest,
by Elsa Beskow • The Pirate Book, by
Lennart Hellsing

CRITICISM

The Streaks of the Tulip, Selected Criticism •
The Spectra Hoax • Herrick, *Selected with
an Introduction and Notes* • Light Verse
and Satires of Witter Bynner, *Edited and with
an Introduction*

ANTHOLOGIES

(with Louise Bogan) The Golden Journey:
Poems for Young People • Poems from
France • Poems from Italy

ARMY BRAT

A MEMOIR BY

WILLIAM JAY SMITH

PERSEA BOOKS 1980 *NEW YORK*

For information, address the publisher:
    Persea Books, Inc.
    225 Lafayette Street
    New York, New York   10012
International Standard Book Number: 0-89255-047-3
Library of Congress Catalog Card Number: 80-82588
Designed by Peter McKenzie
First Edition
Printed in the United States of America

The lines quoted from "Quail in Autumn," "The Barber," and "What Train Will Come" are from *The Traveler's Tree, New and Selected Poems* by William Jay Smith, published by Persea Books, copyright © 1980 by William Jay Smith.

Portions of this book, in slightly different form, appeared in the following periodicals: *The Hudson Review, Nagyvilág* (Budapest), *Shenandoah, PD* (The St. Louis *Post-Dispatch Sunday Magazine*), and *Washington University Magazine* (Washington University in St. Louis).

ACKNOWLEDGMENTS

Bourne Co.: for the lyrics of "Get Out and Get Under the Moon," by Billy Jerome, Charles Tobias, and Larry Shay, copyright © 1928 by Bourne Co. Copyright renewed and assigned to Bourne Co. and Ched Music Corp. Used by permission. And for the lyrics of "Yes, Sir, That's My Baby," by Gus Kahn and Walter Donaldson. Copyright © 1925 by Bourne Co. Copyright renewed and assigned to Bourne Co. and Donaldson Publishing Company. Used by permission.

Chappell & Co., Inc.: for the lyrics of "The Music Goes Round and Around," lyrics by Red Hodgson, music by Edward Farley and Michael Riley, copyright © 1935 by Select Music Publications, Inc. Copyright renewed, all rights administered by Chappell & Co., Inc. (Intersong Music, Publisher). International copyright secured. All rights reserved. Used by permission.

Corvina Press (Budapest): for the quotation from *People of the Puszta* by Gyula Illyés, translated by G.F. Cushing, copyright © 1967 by Corvina. Reprinted by permission.

Farrar, Straus and Giroux: for the stanza of "Ode to Our Young Proconsuls of the Air," from *Collected Poems 1919-1976* by Allen Tate, copyright © 1952, 1953, 1970, 1977 by Allen Tate, copyright © 1931, 1932, 1937, 1948 by Charles Scribner's Sons. Copyright renewed © 1959, 1960, 1965 by Allen Tate. Reprinted by permission.

Leo Feist, Inc.: for the lyrics of "In a Little Spanish Town ('Twas on a Night like This)," words by Sam M. Lewis and Joe Young, music by Mabel Waye, copyright © 1926, renewed 1954 Leo Feist, Inc. All rights reserved. Used by permission. And for the lyrics of "Ramona," words by L. Wolfe Gilbert, music by Mabel Waye, copyright © 1926, renewed 1954 Leo Feist, Inc. All rights reserved. Used by permission.

New Directions: for "Thousand-and-First Ship," stanza four, by F. Scott Fitzgerald ("Jingles and Songs") in *The Notebooks* by F. Scott Fitzgerald, copyright © 1934 by Esquire, Inc., copyright © 1945 by New Directions. Reprinted by permission of New Directions and Harold Ober Associates.

The Sheep Meadow Press: for the lines from "Soldiers Bathing" by F.T. Prince, from *Collected Poems* by F.T. Prince, published by the Sheep Meadow Press, copyright © 1979 by F.T. Prince. Reprinted by permission.

Signal Press: for the selection from *Approved Selections*, National Woman's Christian Temperance Union.

Warner Bros. Music: for the lyrics of "Ain't She Sweet?", lyrics by Jack Yellen, music by Milton Ager. Copyright © 1927 Warner Bros., Inc. Copyright renewed. All rights reserved. Used by permission.

To
my mother
GEORGIA ELLA GUNN
on her eightieth birthday
and to
the memory of my father
JAY SMITH
Corporal, United States Army
1891–1974

CONTENTS

ILLUSTRATIONS

(following page 118)

1. Jefferson Barracks in 1841, from *The Valley of the Mississippi*, by J.C. Wild (St. Louis, 1841). Photograph courtesy of Missouri Historical Society, St. Louis, Mo.
2. Friday afternoon review at Jefferson Barracks in the thirties; the Hospital in the background and the barracks, including the Band Barracks, to the left.
3. The Third U.S. Cavalry Band, stationed at Jefferson Barracks from 1894 to 1898. Photograph courtesy of Jefferson Barracks Museum.
4. The Sixth Infantry Band in the early thirties. My father is the second from the right in the second row.
5. Members of the Sixth Infantry at the rifle range at Arcadia, Missouri, in the thirties. Sgt. Boyd E. Layton, the mess sergeant of Service Company, is kneeling beside the baskets of grapes.
6. Regimental review, Sixth Infantry, at Jefferson Barracks following presentation of the Distinguished Service Cross to Capt. George O. Vonland (second from left), June 2, 1934. Colonel Krueger, commanding officer of Jefferson Barracks, (left), Maj. Tadeo Terriagaki, Japanese exchange officer (second from right), Captain Irwin (far right). Photograph courtesy of Jefferson Barracks Museum.

ARMY BRAT

I am always suspicious of those who harp too much on their "roots," especially before they have displayed the products of those roots. When storks return in the spring, they fly straight as an arrow across whole continents, then circle for hours over their old nests before they finally settle down. What holds them back? They examine every twig in the nest. This is how I too came back and examined the haunts of my childhood: to what end will become clear.
—Gyula Illyés, *People of the Puszta*, translated by G.F. Cushing

I am my memory.
—Saint Augustine

One of my early childhood memories is of a picnic at one corner of the parade ground at Jefferson Barracks, Missouri, on the edge of the Mississippi, just south of St. Louis. An old friend of my mother's is visiting from the South with her small daughter, and we have just taken them on a tour of the Barracks and have had our picnic lunch on an Army blanket spread out on the grass. My mother is wearing a hat that is my favorite, one with a high crown on which red and blue feathers are brushed sideways around it rather than standing up as feathers usually do. It is as if birds of the brightest and softest plumage were circling her head in steady flight. My brother and I have on our short black trousers with the pongee blouses that my mother has made; each of us has also a black straw hat with an elastic under the chin. Off in the distance, led by the band in which my father is playing his clarinet, soldiers are marching up and down. The day is filled with gaiety and pomp and color. While the ladies talk and laugh in their birdlike way, we children run endlessly about. Finally the sun begins to set, the bugle sounds retreat, and still we stay on. As it slowly gets dark I find myself chasing my black hat across the grass. Dark surges suddenly in and the hat's black shiny edges merge with the dark edge of the parade ground. I have a moment of panic, feeling that the hat will just go on circling through the dark to the very end of the parade ground, over the high bluff, and into the wide and muddy river. I put out my hand—almost miraculously it seems—to the exact spot where it is.

Now as I reach back in memory through the darkness of many years I shall try with patience to find the shining edges of that world, lost like the hat, touch them, and bring them back once more—if concentration and luck will allow—to their proper place.

I grew up an Army brat, indelibly marked by my youthful association with my father's profession. As a corporal in the Sixth Infantry Band, my father was not transferred regularly from one post to another, and so, unlike many Army brats, I do not have a patchwork of memories of various posts scattered across the country and around the world, but a single vision of the twenty years spent in and around a particular one, Jefferson Barracks, then a post of major importance. I went there with my father, my mother, and my brother not long after World War I and left at the time of our entry into World War II. It is to those years between the two wars—1921 to 1941—and to my life with the peace-time, "brown-boot" Army that I wish now to turn.

PART ONE

The army is a nation within the nation.... Everyday words sometimes have highly appropriate connotations. To obey or command in an army is indeed to *serve*. We must deplore the servitude, but we should admire the slaves.

— Alfred de Vigny, *The Military Condition* (*Servitude et Grandeur Militaires*, 1835), translated by Marguerite Barnett

1

IN THE EYE
OF THE HURRICANE

"It's time to go to the Mess Hall," my mother
said.

"Georgia, that sounds *dirty!*" said my Aunt
Lucinda, and she laughed until her whole body shook.

Aunt Lucinda, my mother's youngest sister, was
dark and plump with hair tar-black, high cheekbones,
and eyes that rolled like black olives. She had come up
from Arkansas and worked in the telephone company
in East St. Louis. She was an animated Kewpie doll,
but one with black, black hair and deep olive skin.
Even her laughter had a dark, fat, velvety texture.

"Don't be silly," my mother said. "That's what
it's called—the *Mess Hall!* So come along."

Along we went to our annual Thanksgiving dinner
at Atkinson Hall, the huge mess hall located near the
center of Jefferson Barracks. Of concrete painted
white, it stood out in contrast to the brick barracks
surrounding it. When it was first built shortly after

7

our arrival in 1921, the old Mess Hall, known as "Cockroach Bogey," had been abandoned and made available for entertainment. Entertainment at the time was simple; one form was roller skating. The old hall provided, if nothing else, a vast floor space, and someone had the notion to purchase five hundred pairs of roller skates. Skating sessions were held on the main floor and later in the basement. What a sight they must have been, those hundreds of soldiers, whose lives were already regimented and running on grooved rollers, roaring around "Cockroach Bogey" as if their rollered lives had jumped their grooves and were released in a kind of mad rush around and around and around!

The Post Mess Hall was the focal point of life at the Barracks as I was to know it in the twenties and thirties, especially at Thanksgiving and Christmas. The married soldiers and their families along with their guests were then invited to real feasts. There were the traditional holiday fixings—turkey with stuffing, sweet potatoes, cranberry sauce, mince and pumpkin pies—but there were always two items that made the meals special: the long pans of baked beans and the corn bread. The Boston baked beans, first boiled and then seasoned with brown sugar and molasses, ketchup, mustard, and onions and baked with strips of bacon and ham, had, in their pans two or three inches deep and three feet long, the look of mahogany and an aroma that brought all the richness of the autumn woods right into the room. The corn bread, in accompanying pans, had the flavor of corn baked in husks and pulled from a glowing wood fire. The best cooks on the post were Southerners, to whom cooking came naturally, and they had been brought up making the dishes that they served. Some of them went to their graves jealously guarding, even from their own families, the recipes for the barbecue sauce they offered the mess. Guests at these communal gatherings were always provided with a typed—often even a printed—menu. On one of these the Commanding Officer wrote: "When you think of an Army post you must remember that we are really a small town," and then he listed all the services that made Jefferson Barracks a self-sufficient village, right down to the "Army finance officer—our banker."

These meals were times when all members of the garrison were brought together like one great family. Another such time was, of course, Christmas Eve. Then at the Post Chapel the married men and their families would gather for the distribution of presents. The old Chapel, a large frame building painted green, resembled in an odd way a great riverboat that had been beached in the woods. The Mississippi River, in any case, was never far away. It was a terrifying force, always there, always ready to rise up beyond its banks, over the wasteland of the railroad tracks, right up to the entrances of the limestone caves in the hillside above, which had been blackened by the fires of hoboes who had spent the night. My mother, when momentarily overcome by some trying situation, would say, "I'm going to walk to the river till my hat floats!" And I grew up thinking that was the way people coped with difficult situations in life. I could see a great variety of hats of all shapes and sizes floating down that giant, mud-thick river, along with chicken coops and houses.

The faded blue-green Chapel consisted of one large auditorium with a stage so high that those seated below it could see only the feet of those standing above, unless they craned their necks up toward the ceiling.

The Chapel had originally been an all-purpose theater and assembly hall during World War I. Now the beaver board that covered its interior was streaked with great wet spots that looked like fungi attacking it. Church services were held in a small alcove in the rear where there was an upright piano, and Sunday School classes occupied various corners of the rambling structure. One of the first chaplains I knew was Chaplain Jones, an amiable man, whose wife, when she played the piano each Sunday, wore a bright chiffon dress of pink, red, or green with a matching hat of the same fluffy stuff. She carried a large billowing matching handkerchief that would rest on the edge of the piano keys after she had finished her hymn. Big-bosomed, with pearls, she seemed an exotic bird that had come to rest there against the dark wood in the drab interior. When Mrs. Jones put down her handkerchief, we would put down our hymn books—the blue-gray Army and Navy Hymnals that seemed as heavy as slabs of granite but contained, I discovered, any number of musical treasures beneath their eagle-embossed covers. "Onward, Christian Soldiers" was a constant favorite.

> Christ, the royal Master
> Leads against the foe:
> Forward into battle
> See his banners go

we sang until the rafters shook.

On Christmas Eve, the Chapel, heated by pot-bellied stoves, would be packed with every married man on the post, from the highest rank to the lowest, and all his children big and small perched one on top of the other like fruit pouring from a horn of plenty, all the round faces straining to watch for the arrival of Santa Claus. (That role was always taken by the same hefty, pink-cheeked bachelor sergeant, an old Army hand, who enjoyed every minute of it.) He would come into the hall, blowing, snorting, laughing, and stride up to the stage, where he would stand, a giant of a man on a platform close to heaven, beside the great dazzling tree that seemed ready to burst blazing through the roof and carry us off through the sky. Beside him stood a wee, wizened private like a uniformed dwarf, calling out the names of each child as he made his way up—or was lifted up over the beaming faces—to the stage to receive his gift. On these communal occasions rank was forgotten: we were all one family, blessed with bounty.

These were great occasions, but most of the time nothing whatever happened, and even the slightest break in the routine became a dramatic event of importance. An Army post in the twenties and thirties was one of the most boring places on earth, and there were few connections with the outside busy civilian world. One of the most popular songs of the thirties was "The Music Goes Round and Around":

> I push that first valve down,
> And the music goes down and around
> Whoa - ho - ho - ho - ho
> And it comes out here.

When it was discovered that the brother-in-law of one of the staff sergeants at Jefferson Barracks had composed the lyrics to this song, the family became famous overnight—famous, that is, within the confines of the garrison. But that is where we were, even though as children we went off each day—transported in World

War I liberty trucks—to school in South St. Louis. The music went round and round, always the same. And yet I was never bored: even the endless silence that surrounded the routine band music or the bugle calls morning and evening had its own rhythm if you listened carefully. I realize now that as the progeny of the protectors, we were ourselves protected—swept along in the claws of the emblematic eagle we found emblazoned all about us—soaring in the eye of the hurricane between two world wars.

The woods on the reservation were a child's paradise; we knew every inch of these acres: here we followed the fern-lined muddy streams to our swimming holes, fished for crawfish with strips of bacon fat, and on the banks built our tree houses and lean-tos of sassafras in air blue with bluebells and heavy with the perfume of sweet william. On the edge of sinkholes on hot summer evenings, we played a game called "statues," which consisted of allowing yourself to be flung by whoever was "it" and holding whatever position you assumed. I can still feel my foot raised, my finger pointing down through the dark—thick and tufted as in the Doré fairytale illustrations I had discovered in school—a messenger sent to show the way down past the flaming branches of fireflies into the mysterious and deepening night.

As children we gathered bittersweet, hazelnuts, and persimmons in the fall and made our way to the Old Rock Spring (later called Sylvan Springs) to spend hours lying and drinking the clear water, watching the waterbugs dart across the surface of the sandy pool. No one had told us that this was where Jefferson Barracks had actually begun when Capt. Stephen Watts Kearny had set up his camp and built the first log houses in 1826. It was the discovery of this spring that assured him that there would be an adequate water supply for a military post. No doubt even before Captain Kearny the Indians had found this a treasured, and even a sacred, place. In finding our way to it, we were turning instinctively to the most ancient part of the reservation.

2

ARRIVAL AT
JEFFERSON BARRACKS

In the fall of 1921 when their regiment at Camp
Pike near Little Rock, Arkansas, broke up, the
men were allowed to transfer either to a camp in the
state of Washington or to Jefferson Barracks, Missouri.
My father's choice was the latter, mainly because it
was nearer the South, nearer home. He was born in
1891 at Gaar's Mill, Louisiana, near Winnfield, in the
central part of the state, and enlisted in the Army
in 1918.

Jefferson Barracks had a distinguished history.
Founded in 1826, it became the Army's first permanent base west of the Mississippi. When Fort Bellefontaine, which had been established in 1805 north of
St. Louis near the confluence of the Missouri and the
Mississippi, had to be abandoned because of frequent
flooding, the Army sought a new post in the area to
guard the great expanse of wilderness acquired with
the Louisiana Purchase. In 1826, hearing that the

Army was in search of a suitable location, the residents of the small village of Carondelet (now part of South St. Louis), hopeful that the Army post would provide a good market for the produce of their small farms, suggested the new site. The spot they offered, reflecting perhaps their poor economic state, was known in the French that most of them still spoke as "Vide Poche" or "Empty Pocket." When the Army inspected the land and found it suitable, eleven representatives of the Village of Carondelet—among them a gentleman with the resounding name of Hyacinthe Pigeon—met with Col. Joshua B. Brant, representing the Army, in the office of the St. Louis County Recorder. As a token payment for the 1702 acres—or 6,000 arpents, as they were called in French—Colonel Brant handed the spokesman for the group a five-dollar gold piece. The final deed stipulated: "Should the ground ever cease to be used for military purposes it shall revert back with all improvements to the villagers." When the post was deactivated over a hundred years later in 1946, this stipulation caused the descendants of the Carondelet villagers to contest the ownership, until the Supreme Court finally ruled in favor of the United States.

Capt. Stephen Watts Kearny, heading four companies of the First Infantry Regiment, arrived on July 10, 1826, to take possession of the post, which was first called "Cantonment Adams," in honor of President John Quincy Adams. On October 23, 1826, however, the name was changed to Jefferson Barracks to honor President Thomas Jefferson, who had died six days before Captain Kearny arrived.

Over the years Jefferson Barracks became the training ground of such prominent military figures as Ulysses S. Grant, Robert E. Lee, Zachary Taylor, and

Jefferson Davis. Expeditions of the Corps of Topographical Engineers set out from it to blaze trails in
the new territory, and the post became the focal point
for forays against the Indians. Lt. Jefferson Davis
escorted Black Hawk, the famous Sac and Fox Chief,
together with his son Naopope (the Prophet), to Jefferson Barracks after his defeat and capture in 1832 near
Bad Axe River. Black Hawk praised the courtesy
shown them by Davis, whom he described as "a good
and young chief in whose conduct I am much pleased."
When George Catlin came to the Barracks to paint
portraits of Black Hawk and his son, Naopope raised
his ball and chains above his head and exclaimed,
"Paint me thus and show 'the Great Father.'" When
Catlin painted Black Hawk, he was dressed, in Catlin's
words, "in a plain suit of buckskin, with strings of
wampum in his ears and on his neck." In his hand he
held his medicine bag "which was the skin of a black
hawk, from which he had taken his name, and the tail
of which made him a fan, which he was almost constantly using." Washington Irving visited Jefferson
Barracks while Black Hawk was a prisoner and wrote
to a friend: "I find it extremely difficult, even when
near the seat of action, to get at the right story of these
struggles between the white and the red men, and my
sympathies are strongly with the latter." An advertisement published on August 1, 1833, in the *Missouri
Republican* called for recruits for a new regiment of
dragoons being formed at Jefferson Barracks "for the
more perfect defence of the frontiers."

A visitor to Jefferson Barracks in 1827–1828 gave
the following description of life there: "The soldiers
lived in huts and tents, protected by long fences in
front. One of the regiments was in cantonment [tem-
porary barracks] on the south side of the first hill. On

the crest of the hill were extensive stone barracks in progress. Lower down were encamped the first Infantry, some staff and other officers with their families. They occupied huts in very detached situations. The tedium of existence was only enlivened by the music of a full band, the musicians occupying what, by comity, was called the 'grand parade,' shaded by venerable trees. By Christmas the Sixth Infantry got into stone barracks, yet unfinished and uncomfortable. On the eighth of January the First Regiment gave a splendid ball in an unfinished barrack. There was a display of flags and hundreds of bright muskets, with a candle in the muzzle of each, furnishing the needed illumination. The elite from St. Louis and Louisville were present, and beauty added its spell to the charming scene."

Among the famous residents of Jefferson Barracks was Dred Scott, the slave who came there with his master, Dr. John Emerson, an Army surgeon. After Emerson's death in 1843, Dred Scott sued for his freedom and won it ten years later, his suit setting in motion a chain of events that led eventually to the signing of the Emancipation Proclamation.

In 1860 there was hardly a regiment in the entire Army that had not served some time at Jefferson Barracks. During the Civil War, it became the largest Union general hospital. The injured were brought to the post by riverboat and train, and the Western Sanitation Division, forerunner of the American Red Cross, got its start there.

Guns from the bluffs of the post fired holes in the smokestack of a steamboat running the Civil War blockade. One of the passengers on board was Samuel Clemens (Mark Twain), from Hannibal, Missouri, who had enlisted in the Confederate Army, but dropped out not long afterward, weary, as he said, "from constant retreating."

Jefferson Barracks was a staging area in 1898 for Missouri volunteers for the Spanish-American War. A regiment of black soldiers, organized at the post in 1898, was known as the Seventh Regiment of Immunes because blacks were supposed to be immune to yellow fever of which there were epidemics in Cuba and Puerto Rico. These troops got no farther than Macon, Georgia, where they were mustered out in February 1899.

On March 1, 1912, Albert Berry made the first successful parachute jump ever, landing on a chilly afternoon in the middle of the parade ground at Jefferson Barracks. From a pusher-type aircraft, piloted by Anthony Jannus and built by Tom Benoist of St. Louis, Berry jumped from an altitude of 1500 feet. For his jump Berry wore a heavy rubber knee-length coat, cavalry trousers, and boots. He wore a headpiece resembling a football helmet, with a long stocking pulled down over his ears, and auto goggles covering his eyes. A galvanized tin container holding the parachute was strapped to his back.

During World War II Jefferson Barracks served as the Army Air Corps' largest technical training base in the nation. On June 30, 1946, its long service to the United States came to an abrupt end when the Army Service Forces in Washington, declaring it "in the category of surplus," deactivated it permanently.

When we arrived in 1921, the garrison's 1702 acres were mostly finely wooded land with the headquarters building located at the highest central point. Behind it a cannon from the Spanish-American War pointed out toward the river. The barracks buildings, flanking headquarters and lining the parade ground to the south, had been constructed at the turn of the century of the same uniform dark red brick. It is said that everything in nature reverts to magenta, and the bricks of Jefferson Barracks seemed to have reverted, if not to magenta, then to something very close. Was it time or monotony that had darkened them? They were all like so many firehouses one after the other— the same cement steps leading up to the same cement porch, the same iron railing circling each porch, all painted dark green, the companies with lettered designations, A, B, C, D, E, F, along the parade ground, which was trim and immaculate, like a golf course.

The monotonous row of barracks was broken at one point by the ensemble of the guardhouse, the theater, which later served also as a chapel, and the post exchange. Facing the company buildings and fashioned of the same dull brick were the officers' quarters. In the center of Officers' Row stood the Officers' Club with its tennis courts. The officers' quarters were indistinguishable from the company buildings. They were relieved by a little planting before them, and, of course, differentiated from one another by the names of the occupants, each name with its accompanying rank carefully lettered black on white and placed on the top step just below the porch. These quarters were two-story duplexes with screened-in front porches separated from each other by green latticework; each had its bit of carefully tended lawn, its uniform garages behind. Off from the garages stretched the wild acres of the reservation with oak, hickory, and sycamore trees.

Over a wooded area made up of sinkholes and limestone caves were spread the quarters of warrant officers, square brick structures or long wooden ones, the cantonment buildings constructed for troops during

World War I and refashioned into quarters. Each set of quarters had its occupant and his rank designated in black and white lettering like the officers'—right down to the few meager privates who managed to live in quarters at all.

We arrived in 1921, several days in advance of the Sixth Infantry, which my father was to join. On the evening of November 3, 1921, after a nine-hundred-mile hike from Camp Jackson, South Carolina, with the men carrying full packs, the regiment marched into Jefferson Barracks. For the unit, whose motto, "Remember your regiment," had been spoken by Lt. Col. Abner R. Thompson at the Battle of Okee-chobee Swamp in the Seminole War, the return was something of a homecoming. The Sixth Infantry had erected the first permanent buildings at Jefferson Barracks in 1827. The regiment was created in 1798, only to be disbanded two years later and reactivated in 1808. It served in many battles in the War of 1812 and then merged with five other regiments on what became its official birthday, May 17, 1815. After long years of Indian warfare, it always returned to Jefferson Barracks. It fought in a number of battles in the Civil War, marched to the Mexican border in 1914, and then on November 4, 1918, crossed the River Meuse in France and helped break the German line. The Sixth Infantry was the first regiment to enter occupied territory after the Armistice in 1918, and afterward it returned to Camp Gordon, Georgia.

For the men the arrival at Jefferson Barracks that November evening was the end of a long journey and of a long and exacting day. They had left Jones Park in East St. Louis early that morning to pass in review, together with the American Legion, before the mayor of St. Louis and his distinguished guests, General Pershing and Marshal Foch. General Pershing, originally from Missouri, was delighted to welcome the leader of the Allied Forces in World War I on his first visit to the United States. The men of the Sixth Infantry entered Missouri over Eads Bridge at ten-thirty in the morning. But because of a misunderstanding the regiment had crossed the bridge too soon, and the soldiers had to stand in line for an hour and a half stretched from Broadway and Washington Avenue across the bridge. William Friendly, the secretary of Mayor Kiel, greeted Col. Hunter B. Nelson, the commander of the Sixth Infantry, from the steps of a limousine on Washington Avenue: "You have come to a land of plenty and you have not come under arms." When General Pershing later presented Colonel Nelson to Marshal Foch, the Marshal said: "The fine, fresh appearance of his men after so long a march is characteristic of the American Army, and . . . it is an honor to review such a splendid unit."

Two days before, in Kansas City, together with Lieutenant General Baron Jacques of Belgium, General Diaz of Italy, and Admiral of the Fleet Earl Beatty of Great Britain, Marshal Foch had reviewed the men of the American Legion at what was the climax of the Legion's national convention. Legion officials called their parade the greatest procession of marching men in this country since President Lincoln reviewed the victorious Union armies. One of the special and unusual events of the day was the presentation, by the Montana delegation, of a baby wild cat, brought by a committee from Miles City. While the wild kitten squirmed, clawed, and spat in the Marshal's arms, the Montana delegates produced cowboy revolvers and put on a Wild West demonstration. Bewildered, the Marshal turned to General Pershing to ask what was going on.

The Sixth Infantry looked less splendid when a

reporter for the St. Louis *Post-Dispatch* visited it in East St. Louis on November first. It had recently rained, and outside the "squatty, brown burrows" of their pup tents, alongside which "the higher tents of the company Captains and Lieutenants loom big," the men were sloshing around in the mud preparing for the march: "Attired in uniforms of varying degrees of completeness, men all over the camps are busy washing those pieces of clothing they are not wearing in 100 metal tubs and rubbing them on eighty scrub boards furnished by the city of East St. Louis.... The officers too are getting their things cleaned, but it is their 'dog robbers' as the Army refers to officers' servants, who do the worrying for them.... The company field kitchens and muleless escort wagons for supplies are scattered about. Picket lines for the seventy-nine riding horses and 211 mules are established beyond the camp proper.... Rags and puddles of soapy water are everywhere. Sparks fly from the little farrier's shed, where all the animals are being rough shod to prevent their slipping on the St. Louis asphalt." The horses and mules were being groomed; the rolling kitchens were getting a final gloss from a mixture of lampblack and vinegar. The men were also shining their howitzers, machine guns, and Stokes mortars, and greasing the hob-nailed shoes that had carried them over the Cumberland mountains.

A good part of the regiment's spit and polish was gone by the time it arrived at the foot of Broadway at the North Gate of Jefferson Barracks late in the day. Watching them complete their exhausting cross-country trek were my father, my mother, my brother, and I. I was then three and a half years old, and my brother, Earl Richard "Richie," two.

For the first time in weeks the men slept that night

in steam-heated barracks. There were now more than a thousand men at the garrison, including eight hundred in the Sixth Infantry. The next day, Friday, November 4, 1921, was the third anniversary of the regiment's crossing of the Meuse. The men received their October pay just after noon and were granted liberty for the weekend. It was their first opportunity in a very long time to spend any of their money, and a good many people were waiting in the vicinity to help them spend it.

3

PAYDAY

The forbidding and yet enchanting domain of Jefferson Barracks was not to be mine for some time. A few of the lowest ranks among the enlisted men were assigned quarters only after they spoke to their company commanders and asked for them. But it was not my father's nature to ask for anything. And so we went to Lemay, bordering the Barracks on the north, unrelieved by any of the splendid vegetation that the Barracks possessed and made up of mostly unpaved or semi-paved streets, outhouses, and open sewers.

We ended up a few blocks from the North Gate in a row of three-room frame houses all exactly alike. Once white, they were now gray and grimy, separated from each other by picket fences that kept the dogs and children from each others' throats. Our street— suitably called Smith Avenue (now Linn Avenue)— consisted of a long block of the same two-family frame houses, those on one side of the street matching those on the other. Our house had a small front porch, a side porch, a front room, and a back room that opened into a kitchen stretching across the entire back of the house. Under the kitchen was a basement with the only water tap. Back of the kitchen was a small porch that extended from the basement wall. My brother and I played under this porch to escape the sun that beat down unremittingly during the summer. Here we made mud pies that we passed through the picket fence to the girls in the next yard. One of my clay creations was a small human head that for some mysterious reason I painted in its entirety a bright blood-red. It became my most prized possession, a kind of numinous miniature totem that I carried everywhere.

Water had to be brought up from the basement in pitchers and buckets. My mother washed dishes in a large pan, and we all took baths in a galvanized tub. Our furnishings were minimal, but from the people leaving the house we bought a number of objects, including two more modern and comfortable beds to replace the brass ones we had brought up from Arkansas. We acquired a stove with a compartment on the side for heating water which replaced a smaller stove we moved to the basement for heating wash water. The most unusual item—especially for my brother and me—was a phonograph with a few records, mainly of John McCormack. We would climb on chairs, crank the phonograph, and listen by the hour. Another item was a dark maroon china closet, which had originally been a food safe, with tin covering the openings. My father removed the tin and replaced it with glass, but very soon some of the glass got broken and was never replaced. I was always frightened by this dark object, which, like our lives, seemed to have come from nowhere and to be patched up and barely held together.

Smith Avenue was a cul-de-sac, and in a large house at the end, perched over a sinkhole, lived a plump Italian who owned at least a hundred hogs. He was one of the biggest bootleggers in the county, and he fed the remains of his sour mash to his hogs. To keep down the flies, my mother would regularly wash the screens on our windows and doors with Lysol. Also at the end of the street, in a fine house, lived a prosperous German who owned most of the other houses, several of which were occupied by his sons. He would go downtown early in the morning and return with a truck laden with fruits and vegetables which he would market from door to door. He kept chickens and my mother would buy one when she got hold of the money. But that was not often; my father kept control of the purse strings.

There was not much money anywhere at this time, and the regular enlisted man was paid what seems a pittance. A private received a base pay of twenty-one dollars a month—plus clothing, food, and medical care. My father was now one step higher up the ladder; he was a corporal and would retain that rating for most of his twenty-seven years in the Army. He was reduced —busted—several times to private, so that it was one step forward and one step back for him during all his years of service. A corporal's base pay at this time was forty-two dollars a month, with slight increases over the next few years. As a corporal, my father also received a food allowance—ration or subsistence money—amounting to sixteen to eighteen dollars a month. He also had the right to purchase food at the Commissary, and this made all the difference. There he could obtain freshly baked bread for two cents a loaf, a whole side of bacon for fifty cents, a whole ham for little more than a dollar. At the Commissary food was sold at wholesale prices: canned goods for five or six cents a can, a hundred-pound sack of potatoes for a dollar, a seven- or eight-pound roast for about sixty cents, chickens for thirty cents apiece. For two dollars a man could buy more food than he could carry home.

One of the pleasantest smells of my childhood was that of freshly baked bread from the Barracks Bakery. My father would come in at noon, usually with four large loaves wrapped in thick brown paper and tied neatly with a string. The smell would permeate the entire house. Even the paper and the string that bound it gave off a rich aroma. Breast-shaped, the large loaves were still warm from the oven. The outside was brown and crisp, the crust a special delight. The inside was soft and fluffy, but the heel was the best part of all. There was something ritualistic about the delivery of the bread: all the troubles of life vanished before its aroma and its taste. My mother's clean kitchen, where every board and utensil had been rubbed for hours to remove any odor, was suddenly flooded with the richness of life.

In the large brown bag or "shack sack," as the men sometimes termed it, were flour, dried apples from which my mother made tarts and pies, as well as items from the Post Exchange—like the large cakes of laundry soap, good for any number of washes, no fancy wrappings enclosing them, just plump yellow bars that looked like unevenly cut strips of Mississippi mud.

In addition to these supplies available at what seemed below regular wholesale prices, enlisted men like my father could go to a picture show for five cents. The streetcar that took him to and from the Barracks—although much of the time he walked— clanged along for approximately a mile through the woods; the fare was ten cents for adults and five cents for children.

A ride on this streetcar, the Dinkey, or Toonerville Trolley, was a thrill in itself. At the end of Broadway next to the North Gate of the Barracks it veered straight into the woods, a roller coaster right through the wilderness. For ten minutes there was no sign of civilization whatever: the little trolley swung like a bucket through the trees, picking up all the freshness as it went. The cardinals that flashed through the branches seemed to come in at the windows: you could reach out and pick blackberries along the way. At night the trip was even more mysterious: the owl-haunted darkness closed around the yellow jangling box of the trolley like a giant's palm and hurled it straight ahead.

The rent of our house on Smith Avenue was fifteen dollars a month, and with the subsistence allowance we were able to scrape by—that is, if my father's monthly pay arrived home intact. But that was rarely the case: he would sometimes bring home as much as a hundred times his pay; at other times he would arrive without a cent. The reason was quite simply poker. When payday arrived, poker games proliferated like bonfires throughout the post, and my father was one of the most intense and devoted players. Gambling was a passion with him. He would curse it at times as a vice that ought to be kept under control; at others, he enjoyed it as if nothing else in the world existed. As a young man off the farm in Louisiana, he learned poker during his five-year hitch in the Navy and mastered the game sufficiently so that at the end of his enlistment he was several thousand dollars ahead, enough to purchase a bar on the Embarcadero—the Gold Coast —in San Francisco. When he had drunk up his profits, he sold out and returned to the farm in Louisiana. It was on his way there that he stopped off at Pine Bluff, Arkansas, to visit his brother's widow and to marry her sister, my mother.

Gambling has always been endemic with the military, but on an Army post in the twenties it was a way of life. Every company building had its day room where the men could play pool or cards. Playing for money on the premises was, of course, against Army regulations, but since the officers themselves were gambling at the officers' club, they closed their eyes to the whole thing. To attempt to do otherwise would probably have been impossible anyway, because as soon as a game was closed up in one place another would immediately spring up elsewhere.

The stakes were often high in both poker and crap games. One roll of the dice in a Service Company crap game would sometimes be for as much as $1,000. On maneuvers like those in 1934 at Camp Custer, Michigan, almost the entire regimental payroll would be on the blanket at one time. One of the top gamblers on the post, a Bandsman who averaged $1,000 a month from poker, tried to get transferred to Schofield Barracks, Hawaii, because the stakes there were said to be the highest anywhere. Every month the routine was much the same: the big winners in each company would move on to the basement of Headquarters Barracks near the stables for a final game.

If there were big winners, there were also big losers. Jawboning—living on credit—was an ancient tradition in the Army, and most enlisted men jawboned from month to month, hoping with each payday to recoup their losses. Loan sharks would advance them money at twenty-five percent interest. Or they could trade the canteen checks they drew for cash, but these would bring only half their value, and the little cash they received would also soon disappear. Or they would hock what was left of their civilian clothing at a pawnshop a few miles from the post, where it would usually remain unclaimed.

The company barracks had endless little rooms, one like the next, and on payday there were usually several games going on even in the same company: in the smoke-filled rooms the men in khaki would hunch over the green baize of the gambling table while a green lamp hung from the ceiling, its circle of light drinking in the colors of the chips and the green of the folding money.

Green was certainly the thematic color of the post, beginning in spring with green sweeping over the hills of the reservation, settling in stagnant pools at the bottoms of the sinkholes and in patches of May apples under the oaks, reaching its height in the summer when the parade ground shimmered like an emerald, its green glow cool to the touch in the terrible heat. Dark blue-green paint was everywhere—in the trim of the buildings, on the benches, the fences, the lawn chairs; the khaki of the uniform was of a far greener tint than that worn later in World War II; the leggings the men wound around their legs resembled strips of freshly cut turf. And green also were the O.D. (olive drab) Army blankets that enshrouded every bed in every barracks, their corners squared away, the same blankets that found their way into the homes of the officers and enlisted men—covering their beds, spread out on their lawns, carried on picnics into the woods, to summer camps on the Meramac and the Gasconade Rivers, blankets that covered the backs of their horses, that their children wore cut into coats for winter or flung over them for tents or lean-tos in the summer on the edges of the muddy creeks. Green, which in its ever-renewed subtle variations, is the color of life itself, became the color of monotony, of suffocation. And at the core of this monotony was the green of the gambling table where the green figures of the men like alchemists attempted to change the dull base green of their daily lives into gold.

To me the central alchemist was my father, a magician capable of great good feats and of evil deeds as well. Sometimes in the evening he would spread a blanket on our kitchen table and sit by the hour simply shuffling, dealing, and redealing the cards. There is no sound in the world like the shuffling of a deck of cards: it combines the clicking and tapping of the opening and closing of a fan with the rolling of drums; there is something both delicate and deafening about it. It is a kind of slow, exquisite, hypnotic torture, allowing the gambler to touch fate, deciding both his future and that of his opponent by the subtle movement of his fingers. To the confirmed player the successive rufflings of the cards as they fall one on the other must be like the fingertips working with all the nerves in the body the combination of a safe or moving up and down the keyboard to release the most marvelous hidden harmonies. My father had mastered the art of dealing: his hands weaving back and forth like shuttles, he could whip out a card from the center of the deck or deal another from the bottom without the observer having any idea where they had come from. They might look as if they came tumbling from his sleeves; they did not. He used none of those mechanical devices belted around the body and attached to the sleeves, and with the serge shirt that he usually wore they would have been impossible in any case.

His success he owed to what he called "psychol-

ogy." He would study the expressions on the faces of
the other players and tell what they were holding in
their hands. Psychology, however, was a two-way
street, and I wonder if he didn't fool the other players
most of the time by not revealing anything on his own
face. When he sat immobile, his blue eyes fixed
straight ahead, his jaw squared, his ears tilted out
slightly at the top, there is no doubt that he looked
fierce. His voice, which had not much depth and even
at times went off into a high register, he could maneuver into a kind of evil snarl. And he could clear his
sinuses and his throat with a snort and a roll that
would seem to wake the dead. Often he would be
sitting in a room reading a newspaper. There was not
a sound, and then all of a sudden from behind his
paper would come a terrible snort like a minor earthquake, a great indrawing of breath, a rumble, and a
roar. Then a crash, a crinkling; he would wad up the
paper, hurl it to the floor, and exclaim in a loud voice
as if he were giving orders to a squad of men: *"Bal-
zac!"*

I don't think that he had ever read a word by Bal-
zac. It was just the sound of the word—especially the
first syllable—which made this the fitting exclamation
to conclude whatever had been going through his head.

In early photographs, posing with his Winnfield,
Louisiana, high school baseball team or holding his
clarinet as a young and handsome man in the Navy
band, my father already had an intent look, a stony
gaze.

Years later he was sitting one morning in a diner
having breakfast and next to him sat a pretty young
woman. When the pancakes she ordered arrived, she
daintily touched them with butter and then picked up
the jug that held the syrup. The top was the sort that
slides back and frequently gets stuck with the syrup.

32

And this is what happened: holding the jug above her plate and pointing it in the direction of my father, she pulled the top back until it suddenly came unstuck and released a heavy stream of syrup directly into his face. The young woman was too horrified and embarrassed at first to move, but then finally, close to tears, she exclaimed, "Oh, I'm so *sorry!*"

Without moving a muscle in his face, the syrup still streaming down on his clothes, my father gazed back at her.

"You goddam well ought to be!" he said.

The young woman then dissolved completely in tears and made her way unsteadily toward the door, her pancakes untouched.

My father had the general physiognomy and stance of a fighter—and he had indeed boxed while in the Navy. His jaw was firm, and his hair, light brown when he was young and graying in his forties, was always kept closely cropped, so that the cowlick that emerged above his right eye was not permitted to complete its wave but was chopped off like a cockscomb. His ears were a boxer's ears, not big cauliflower ones, but small and tilted out at the top, so that they looked as if they had been pushed down under a hat that had just been removed.

At the poker table his fierce look apparently caused strong constitutions to collapse, to abandon their hands and pay up. But it was not infallible. His look was sometimes returned from the other side of the table, and luck was not always kind. Payday—at the end of each month—meant not only waiting for Daddy to come home but also wondering what he would bring. The men were paid in the morning and the poker games usually began at ten o'clock. On ordinary days my father would appear at lunch time with great brown bags of commissaries and loaves of fresh bread.

Unless he was on guard duty or unless there was a parade, as there always was on Friday afternoon, his main duties were frequently finished for the day.

I could sense that it was payday by the anxiety in my mother's movements. She went about her usual tasks, cleaning, polishing, cooking, sewing, but still my father's absence was like a great black pit into which everything—the room, the house, the beds, the china closet, the cut-glass vase, the stove—was about to shift and sink along with her. And there we were, my brother and I, holding close to her skirts at the edge of the pit, trying to understand.

On payday my father never appeared at noon, never in the afternoon, and sometimes not until late at night or early the next morning. (When the lights went out in the barracks, the poker and crap games would go on in the basements, in the tailor shops, or in the latrines.) If my father did not appear until noon the following day, it was clear that something had gone wrong.

The day finally came when, on the afternoon after payday, my father had still not appeared.

As the hours passed and he was nowhere in sight, my mother dressed my brother and me (I was four years old at the time and my brother, three). She put on our pongee blouses, our short black trousers, our black straw hats, and guiding us one by each hand, she started out in search of my father.

My mother was then a strikingly beautiful woman. Her hair was auburn, a dark copper-red that glistened in the light; she wore it long—she had never cut it— and its waves enclosed her face with its peach-pale skin, high cheek bones, and eyes so black you could scarcely make out where the pupils began or left off. Men and women often stopped to stare at her in the street, as they must have that afternoon. She wore a black taffeta dress with a wide lace collar, that she had just made.

We went to every speakeasy in the county. Dark doors would open; the stale smell of home brew and Bull Durham tobacco would waft out. Faces would rise up through the smoke, and then we would turn back to the hot street, with still no sign of the lost corporal.

My mother said little to us—what was there to say? —but we knew that something was wrong. When we got home toward the end of the afternoon, we discovered, as we approached the house, how wrong it was. The thin gingerbread bannisters of the front porch were riddled with bullet holes. When we opened the screen door, there lay my father sprawled on the living room floor, his pistol at his side.

Scattered all around the room was money, piles of bills, all the green of the gambling tables coming home to roost, and from my father's mouth oozed a foul-smelling, pale green liquid that spread across the floor.

There was a moment of terrible silence like a door flung open into empty and infinite space. Then there was a scream: it felt as if it came right up through the floor on which I stood, rising within me and fountaining out, spreading in every direction like the green ooze on the floor.

My brother began on a higher note, and while the two of us bellowed like wild, wounded animals, my mother managed somehow to get milk and force it down my father's throat and then to get him to bed where she continued to pour milk into him, as she did for the next several days.

She would have him fully recovered and ready for the next payday.

My father had played poker with men who came

out from the city. He went to a place he did not know, and when he had won about $5,000, the men he played with started feeding him rot-gut whiskey, which they doped up. He managed somehow to get away and came back to shoot up the porch and to terrify the neighborhood.

My mother returned to my father most of the bills that she scooped up, but she kept a certain number for herself, and sent several hundred dollars to her eldest sister, my Aunt Effie, a widow with five children on a farm in Arkansas. Effie accepted the money, but in accepting it, she did not forget her Bible-belt background. She sent, along with her acceptance, a long lecture on the evils of gambling.

4

THE GREAT DEPRESSION

The Great Depression began for us a long while before the crash in 1929; I would date it almost from the time of our arrival at Jefferson Barracks in 1921. With money won at the gambling table, my father bought out of the Army in August 1923, six months before his enlistment was up, and for two years tried to make a go of things in civilian life.

While in service he had met a man who sold an all-purpose cleaning powder and who had convinced him that this was an easy, almost effortless way to make a living. My father purchased the cleaner and fashioned it somehow into spheres about the size of tennis balls. Streaked with blue and white, they looked rather like wads of bubble gum stuck together. When he had made enough of them to fill a suitcase, he started off from door to door. After a week or two, with almost all the balls still in his suitcase, he saw that this job was clearly not the way to a quick fortune. Mother, pragmatic as usual, tried out the cleaning balls and found that rather than cleaning everything, they could clean nothing at all.

When the money he had saved from the service had been nearly all used up, my father found an advertisement for the biggest dairy in St. Louis, the Mayfair Dairy, whose yellow wagons were a familiar sight around the city. He went off early the next morning to apply for the job of wagon driver. To his great astonishment he discovered within a day or two that out of several applicants he had landed the job.

His schedule was back-breaking. He had to get up at two thirty in the morning and take the streetcar (about an hour's trip) into St. Louis, hitch up his two horses, load up his wagon, and then begin his tiring round. He would not get back, after a similar streetcar ride, until late in the afternoon.

He told my mother that one of the other drivers explained to him why he kept his job.

"If I don't," the fellow had said, "some son-of-a-bitch will be only too glad to take my place."

After four months, my father said one morning, "This work is too damned hard, and, by God, I *am* going to let some son-of-a-bitch take my place."

And so, in February 1925, he went out to Jefferson Barracks to reenlist for another three years.

My father was not the first soldier in the St. Louis area unable to cope with civilian life. Ulysses S. Grant was assigned to Jefferson Barracks on graduating from the United States Military Academy, and as a handsome, blue-eyed young second lieutenant he played the part of Desdemona in a theatrical production there. He resigned from the Army in 1852 rather than face a court martial for his drinking. He married Julia Dent of St. Louis, the sister of a classmate at West Point, and lived for some time on his father-in-law's farm, five miles west of Jefferson Barracks. He made his living for a while by selling wood to the post. He tried farming and real estate. And when his company of Illinois volunteers was organized at the beginning of the Civil War, he was a clerk in his father's store in Galena, Illinois, a failure in civilian life. William Tecumseh Sherman also tried banking and real estate, and served as superintendent of a military school in Louisiana. He was employed by the builders of the first streetcar line in St. Louis, but drew little more pay than the drivers of the horse-cars of the line. Like Grant he considered himself a failure. The Civil War gave both men a reason for being.

As late as the thirties jobs around St. Louis and in southern Illinois were scarce, and many men, even college graduates, still turned to the Army. James Jones, who later brilliantly chronicled the lives of enlisted men in World War II, could find nothing to do when he graduated from high school in Robinson, Illinois, in 1939. His family lost its house and real estate holdings at the time of Samuel Insull's embezzlement of funds in Chicago. Jones's father, who had a sentimental memory of his service in World War I, suggested that his son join the regular Army. Jones, who in World War II was awarded both the Bronze Star and the Purple Heart, was like my father several times reduced from corporal and sergeant to private. He knew intimately the triumphs and humiliations of the enlisted man who could cope with the civilian world on weekend liberty, but who, if abandoned to it completely, would sink in it as in a swamp.

We had moved in the spring to Teddy Avenue (Roosevelt Place had been its official name originally), a little ragged street that wound down the hill from Broadway, just a block away from the North Gate of the Barracks. Ours was a yellow house surrounded by a big yard—two yards in fact since there was an empty lot next door that was part of the property—with huge trees, tall grasses, and large clumps of violets, more than I had ever seen.

Our house was completely enclosed by fences, and my brother and I were never allowed out of the yard. There was no traffic on the street to worry about; it was rare to see a pedestrian pass by. But my mother did not approve of the neighbors; they were not the type of people she wanted her children to associate with. She had been put off by the sight of our next-door neighbors' yard, a wide and open expanse of mud, filled with dogs and dirty and half-naked children. I saw nothing beyond the fence until September when I began school. I was six years old in April, and since I had heard that you could go to school when you were six, I begged my mother to send me right off.

"You must wait until September," she said.

When September came, I walked each morning up to the corner where the Barracks school bus stopped to pick me up to take me to Hancock School, a few miles up Broadway. I was soon completely absorbed in my studies.

The first book I made at school was composed on pieces of brown wrapping paper in which the bread from the Commissary arrived. From a magazine I cut out a circular picture of a woman who was using a curling iron in front of a mirror, and pasted it on the cover—clearly an impression of my mother. She had been ill with diphtheria before we moved from Smith Avenue and almost died. I could remember being led through her bedroom with a mask over my face. As a result of the disease, her beautiful long auburn hair started to fall out, and she filled whole baskets when she combed it. The sight of the baskets was alarming, but soon her hair was growing back rich and full. My book contained drawings of maple leaves, pumpkins, and pilgrims cut from black paper. Alongside the pilgrims was a whole field of odd-looking four-legged turkeys.

These first months on Teddy Avenue were blissful. I loved school and our cozy house with its luxuriant yard. My father and mother, who were happy together, spent hours encouraging me with my school work. A symbol of this happy time appeared suddenly one day when a handsome brown and white collie followed my father home from the Barracks and insisted on staying with us in our peaceful enclosure. My father was not a lover of animals, but he could not send away this dog, which for some reason had attached itself to him, and clearly seemed to want to share our lives. My mother washed, combed, and brushed the collie, and like a great lion it shared every moment on the grassy slopes with Richie and me. But just as suddenly as it had appeared, it disappeared, managing one day to find a hole in the fence.

Not only did I lose the only dog that I was ever to own as a boy, but I almost lost my life at about the same time. One afternoon while I waited in line to get on a swing at school, a classmate pushed me forward (there were no railings around the swings), and a corner of the steel swing struck me near the right temple. If I had moved just an inch closer, the swing might have killed me on the spot or put out my eye. I was taken to a neighboring doctor's office and after a short rest, my head swathed in bandages, I was permitted to walk home. I had the sensation of having a hole straight through my head, one that I could put my hand right through. My mother almost fainted when she saw me open the front gate.

A few months later we lost the house and yard

when the soldier who owned it returned to the Barracks. Having to leave it was like being driven from paradise. We went to a two-room structure at the bottom of the street, perched high above a sinkhole. All the color went out of our lives: everything here on the street that dead-ended in the sinkhole and a lane known as Tin Can Alley seemed reduced to black and white. It was winter and cold; snow drifted over the high front steps and swept down into the sinkhole. The beds in the front room were covered with white crocheted bedspreads; the whole white world inside, poised against the outer white, was broken by the black of the coal in the scuttle that fed the little stove that kept us warm. The smokestack on top of the house was not high enough, and the wind forced the smoke down into the room. The other black, somber note in this white world was my father's pistol, which he brought forth from its holster sometimes after he had been drinking, and his drinking bouts now became more frequent. The morning after such a pistol-packing bout, he would be his charming, witty self again.

Heavy drinking, like gambling, has always been associated with the military. Colonel George Croghan, a hero of the War of 1812, as Inspector General of the posts in the Mississippi Valley during the 1840's, reported on the drunkenness of the soldiers at Jefferson Barracks. Colonel Croghan himself became a heavy drinker and almost lost his position because of it. In the Army over the years drinking became a matter of pride and a badge of merit, although from time to time attempts were made to form temperance societies. Bartenders near Army posts during World War II were said to be able to tell regular Army men from draftees by the far greater amount of beer the former could consume. My father's drinking had first been confined to paydays, but he was soon drinking at other times, not only to join his fellow Bandsmen but also to relieve the pain brought on by his teeth. He discovered not long after his marriage when his gums began to swell that he suffered from pyorrhea, for which there was no cure at the time. Sooner or later all his teeth would have to go. The gums would swell, the teeth would loosen and drop out. When his front teeth all finally went, he made himself a wooden block bridge that he inserted in order to play his clarinet. But not all the teeth came out easily, and he had to make frequent trips to the dentist, all before the days of advanced dentistry and pain-killers. My father made matters worse by putting off having all his teeth removed, and the delay only increased the pain.

Shortly after quitting his dairy job, more and more despondent over his inability to master the cruel civilian world, he came home drunk one winter day. Snow was falling over the sinkhole, and the room was heavy with the smell of smoke from the black stove. A black cat that had wandered in on us a few days before had left its place beside the stove and had curled up in the middle of the white bed. My father came cursing into the room, picked up the black cat, and hurled it out into the snow. As the cat scurried off like a trail of ink through the snowdrifts, the house with the black, smoking stove, the rickety flue, and the white bedspread seemed to collapse around us and tumble into the sinkhole beside it. We had reached the ultimate edge of the civilian swamp. The next morning my father took up his clarinet and went off to reenlist in the Army for another three years.

Word soon came to men who lived off the post: if they were willing to build their own quarters from beaver board that the Army would supply, they could move into a large red rambling frame structure that had been built by the Knights of Columbus as an auditorium for the soldiers at Jefferson Barracks in World War I. Rather than tear it down, the commanding officer decided to let it be used for quarters. My father, an excellent carpenter, picked out a spot near the woods on one end of the building away from the road and fashioned for us a comfortable and pleasant four-room apartment, the back of which opened into the old stage, which became both a storage place and a playground. It was here in the K.C. Building—as we always called it—that our full Army life began.

5

SPIT AND POLISH

They are covered with countless crosses;
    Plumes of princely types
Like parasitic mosses
    Sweep their campaign stripes.

So begins one of my early poems. The lines were prompted not by any particular officer but probably by the regular Friday afternoon reviews or dress parades that I had watched over the years. On these occasions the entire regiment sparkled as if it had just stepped out of a box of toys on to the green turf of the parade ground.

During the twenties and thirties everything inside and out at Jefferson Barracks looked as if it had just been scrubbed and polished—for the very good reason that it no doubt had been. Nothing was left uncared for, right down to the lowliest mule. Indeed, the mules were the pride of the post. The stables were immaculate, and the mules were so combed and curried by the "mule-skinners" of Service Company that they looked as if they had been groomed for races rather than for their lowly duty of dragging equipment. We were so accustomed to seeing the mules cared for in this fashion that when my brother and I went back to visit my grandmother and aunt and uncle on the farm in Louisiana and were shown my uncle's mule, Richie refused to accept it as such. "That's not a mule," he said, "that's just a donkey!"

Spit and polish—those were the words of the day. And they were even more the words from 1932 to 1934 when Col. Walter Krueger was commanding officer. Born in Prussia, Krueger, at the time the youngest colonel in the service, had come to the United States at the age of eight and had enlisted as a private in the Army at the age of seventeen. He had fought in the Spanish-American War and the Philippine Insurrection, and was decorated for distinguished service at Château-Thierry and in the Meuse-Argonne in France. He became the commanding general of the United States Sixth Army during World War II, the first private to rise to four-star rank. At the end of the war, he had completed plans for the largest amphibious operation in history—an assault on Japan that would have involved 800,000 men—if the dropping of the atomic bomb had not made it unnecessary. Men who served under him at Jefferson Barracks remember his mania for keeping everything trim and neat. He would sneak around, they say, on surprise inspections to every corner of the barracks, into the kitchens and the latrines. The prisoners worked regularly extracting every blade of grass from the blocks of limestone in the gutters along the parade ground, and the men waxed and polished the floors of their barracks. The plain wooden floors were cleaned with sand rock and lye water and then waxed. Johnson's wax was applied with a Johnson bar consisting of a piece of rug wrapped around a weight on a long handle. At a later date the floors were covered with "battleship linoleum," which was one-quarter-inch thick and would not chip or scratch. "Shine the brass!" Colonel Krueger ordered, and every bit of visible brass everywhere would sparkle. Brass cuspidors were placed in the corners of almost every barracks room. Filled with fresh water, they shone, ready for use, but they were never used. They were there for show: cigarettes and cigar butts were thrown in a butt can that was removed and hidden during regular inspections.

There were weekly white-glove inspections not just of the barracks but of the enlisted men's quarters as well. In the K.C. Building, there was always great anxiety on Saturday morning. As the officers made their rounds, there would be knocks of warning on the beaverboard walls separating the quarters to notify the neighbors that the officers were approaching and to give them time to put away their home brew or other unwelcome or unsightly objects.

The brass shone in the enlisted men's quarters as well: the flower vases, fashioned from sawed-off shells, glowed on delicate white doilies that the women had crocheted. The prisoners did the hard work, such as cutting the grass, cleaning the walks, hauling coal, and washing the windows for enlisted men as well as for officers. Such was the attention to cleanliness that the clothes of the lowest enlisted man's children were usually spotless. Even the prostitutes who turned up regularly at noon on payday at the trolley station seemed to have dressed in keeping with the polished look of the post. With frizzled hair showing the recent effect of the hot curling iron and faces heavily made up, they often wore evening dresses of bright red or green satin, but because their assignations were usually somewhere in the woods, they also wore tennis shoes so that they might more readily cope with the difficult terrain.

In addition to the regular inspections of the barracks, there were frequent eight- or ten-mile hikes with full packs and in the summer visits to the rifle range at Arcadia, Missouri, where each man had to qualify. It was to Arcadia that the mules were retired when they became too old for service. The mules were treated like soldiers: each had his serial number (the mule's was branded on his left hip), and like the soldier each one had to be accounted for and provided with a decent retirement. One summer the regiment hiked to Battle Creek, Michigan, for maneuvers, taking twenty-one days and nights. Along with the other constant inspections there were, of course, the routine "short-arm" inspections (for venereal disease). At one such inspection a Bandsman was found to have gonorrhea, but rather than having to pay the usual penalty of being busted and having his pay docked, he was able to beat the system. By asking that she also be examined, he was able to prove that he had contracted the disease from his wife, who had picked it up from another man while her husband was away on the rifle range. The man lost his wife, but kept his rating.

"Shine the brass!" the Colonel ordered, and for a Bandsman like my father there was plenty of brass to shine. A photograph of the Third Cavalry Band in 1894 shows the men in tunics with three rows of buttons and helmets with large metal plaques in front that make them look as if they have just walked off the stage from some comic opera. My father's uniform was not that fancy but it took just as much care. To begin with, every button had to be polished, and as they were heavily embossed, the task took attention and elbow grease. Father's button board from the PX was V-shaped, of heavy cardboard, made to hook around each button. He applied a combination of salt, vinegar, and scrubbing powder, followed by jeweler's rouge, and a final polishing with a Blitz Cloth. (In 1843 a school for infantry brigade drill had been established at Jefferson Barracks, and it was here that the Third Infantry, because of its glittering look on parade, won the nickname of "Buffsticks," from the constant use of just such a slotted button board.)

The brass was quite enough in itself, but the leggings were a real nightmare. The ordinary canvas leggings—puttees—worn in World War I, had been replaced by wool wrap-around leggings, and winding these properly was an art in itself. You had to start from the top of the shoe in just the proper way so that if it rained the water would run off each succeeding layer. In addition, for parades the Band wore white canvas leggings, the strings of which had to be bleached and the brass tips of the strings polished. The leggings themselves had to be scrubbed with brushes. The Band also had to wear white web belts, which the men had to scrub or "blanco" with a Paris-green powder. And every brass eyelet on the belt had to be polished. For this job my father had what was called a "whirligig," in which a polishing surface would descend in whirling yoyo-fashion on each eyelet. This tool did its work so effectively that it was much in demand and was frequently rented out to his fellow Bandsmen.

Special care, of course, had to be taken with rifles. The gunstocks were made to shine like brass. One of the sergeants in B Company was known as "Gunrack" Miller because he was so particular about his rifle that he never wanted to take it from the rack. He would put linseed oil on the gunstock and rub it for hours over and over with the palm of his hand.

Colonel Krueger decided at one point that he did

not like the color of the men's shoes or garrison belts. And soon the order went out for them to be dyed a darker brown. This was not easily accomplished, and it took constant surveillance to keep the results from looking messy.

Ordinarily the men wore a woolen serge uniform in winter, one that had to be cleaned and pressed and kept pressed, with a straight black cotton necktie, and in summer a khaki uniform and a thin khaki necktie. The khakis—or "sun tans"—were, of course, washable, but since they had to be starched, they were not always so easy to handle. Some of the officers, not content with the way the Post Laundry did their khaki trousers, took them to the wives of enlisted men so that they might get special attention. Captain James Piston, a bachelor living at the Officers' Club, sought out Mrs. Velma Gholson, the wife of Sergeant Gholson of B Company. Captain Piston explained to her that he wanted his trousers starched so stiff they would stand up. Mrs. Gholson obliged, but the next week Captain Piston sent a note, saying, "A little more starch, please." Mrs. Gholson increased the amount, and a second note came back, requesting still more starch. The third time she decided to prepare them as she did the nurses' caps, by washing and drying them first and then putting them through hot starch. Captain Piston was delighted and strutted out like a knight who had donned new armor for the weekly review. Unfortunately it rained, and he found himself encased in what amounted to plaster. The following week he sent a final request, "Not quite so much starch, please."

The sun tans, whether starched stiff or not, were at least fairly cool. But Colonel Krueger decided that khaki for summer was messy and that wool was the thing. Although it was warm, it had the advantage of absorbing perspiration, which did not show through until the men were ready to keel over in the hundred-degree heat. The men would return from the Friday afternoon reviews soaked to the skin, and then the woolen uniform would have to be readied for the next day. Colonel Krueger also enjoyed making speeches, and from time to time he would assemble the men of the regiment in the Post Theater and address them on the subject of discipline. "You must learn to be led before you can learn to lead," he would tell them.

While much of a soldier's time was ordinarily spent in carrying out orders, a good amount was also spent in finding ways of not carrying them out or beating the system in one way or another—which under Colonel Krueger became increasingly difficult. The routine of the day went something like this: 5:30 A.M. reveille; 6:00 A.M. breakfast (The Band ate with Service Company); at 7:30 A.M. the entire regiment would line up on the parade ground in undershirts and trousers for half an hour of calisthenics and butts manual; 8:00 A.M. drill call (for the line companies squad drill, for the Band, rehearsal); 11:30 A.M. guard mount (the changing of the guard), which was always held in front of the old H Company on the corner of the parade ground next to the Headquarters Building; 12:00 noon chow (dinner); from 1:00 P.M. to 3:00 P.M. fatigue. (Some men had special assignments and others rested. During this period the old soldiers would stretch out on their bunks, and the young recruits, fearing their wrath and careful not to disturb them, would tiptoe in stocking feet up glossy stairs still smelling from their heavy application of floor wax.) The regiment would fall out about 4:00 P.M. for review for about an hour (or on Friday for the regular weekly review). At 5:00 P.M. retreat sounded. Before Colonel Krueger's time, the Band had not been required to turn out for retreat; a single bugler (buglers were not connected with the Band) had sufficed. But Colonel Krueger decided that the full Band should be present for retreat seven days a week. At 6:00 P.M. chow (supper), followed by 9:00 P.M. tattoo and 10:00 P.M. taps, at which time lights went out except in the latrines and entrances. If poker or crap games were in progress, they moved to the latrines or somewhere like the tailor's shop in the basement that was tucked away from general view—and there they frequently continued all night long.

The daily routine under Colonel Krueger was bad enough, but it was followed, when General Preston D. Brown took over as corps area commander, by what the men called "General Brown's reign of terror." General Brown instituted a nightly bed check at 11:00 P.M. Only married men were exempt and those who tried to avoid it, as one Bandsman did by filling his bed with two hefty barracks bags, were readily apprehended. Two men, speeding back from St. Louis for bed check after a night on the town, wheeled into a sinkhole and were both killed. Bed check was dropped not long afterward.

In one of Bill Mauldin's famous cartoons two generals are shown contemplating a spectacular sunset. "It's a beautiful view," one says to the other. "Is there one for the enlisted men?" If an enlisted man dared to walk out in the company of an officer to look at the sun setting behind the parade ground at Jefferson Barracks at the time that I knew it, he would have had to keep a pace or two to his left and rear. And he would, of course, always have to show the utmost respect in addressing him. An enlisted man was required to give his rating, name, and serial number, and to refer to the officer in the third person. One of the men who served with my father was Pvt.—later, in World War II—Master Sgt. William F. Alden, who became historian of the Sixth Infantry. Like many of the recruits of the day, he came from a small town in southern Illinois. When he first arrived at the post, the men in his squad room found on his bunk his hometown newspaper with an article about him bearing the headline: LOCAL BOY JOINS ARMY. From that day on he was known by all the men as "Local Boy."

Alden recalls going in to see Captain Henderson, the Commanding Officer of Service Company, to request permission to get married.

"Local Boy," standing at attention, said, "Sir, Private William F. Alden, Serial Number 6829056, desires the permission of the company commander to be married on the twenty-eighth day of September 1934, if it so pleases the commanding officer."

"Sit down, Alden," Captain Henderson replied. "You know you're a damn fool. Any man who asks a woman to share the life of the military is a damn fool."

Then, after a long tirade outlining all that Alden would be putting his bride through, he concluded: "I'll send a letter along, and we'll see what we get back." And that meant that there would be no problem.

The regular complement of the Band was twenty-eight men. There was a warrant officer, who was Bandmaster, a first sergeant, a staff sergeant, four sergeants, two corporals, and the others were privates, first, second, third, fourth, fifth, and sixth class. The privates—the "peons" my father called them—had the lowliest duties, K.P. (Kitchen Police) and general policing up. A corporal like my father, in charge of a detail or squad of eight men, would police the peons. Some men like "Local Boy" Alden were members of Service Company but were attached to the Band for duty until a permanent slot opened up. These men often drew duty cleaning up the stables. They would be put on what they called "pilot" detail, which, they said, meant simply "pile it here" and "pile it there."

The instruments for the Bandsmen were furnished, but my father owned his own clarinet. Resting in segments in its royal purple plush-lined case, it received more attention than his rifle. He had learned to play the clarinet in his Winnfield, Louisiana, high school. During his hitch in the Navy he joined the band in order to avoid scrubbing decks. He played well and could have been a really fine musician if he had wanted to. Even with drinking and gambling, he managed to practice regularly.

The notes of the clarinet still have for me a special charm. When I listened while my father practiced in front of his music stand on a still afternoon, his hands moving dextrously up and down the stops, the wind at the window, redolent of the sweet, green woods, seemed itself to be playing the instrument, calling for me to follow to distant fern-enclosed glades and cool limestone caverns.

Gen. George S. Brown, when Chairman of the Joint Chiefs of Staff, remarked that Great Britain was no longer a world power: "All they've got are generals and admirals and bands." The United States has never been lacking in all three. From the beginning bands were an important part of life at Jefferson Barracks, as they had been on all frontier posts. Regulations in 1861 provided for regimental bands and band leaders. Bandsmen in combat were supposed to be litter-bearers, but more often they played to bolster the morale of the forces. When General Custer and his troops marched off from Fort Lincoln, North Dakota, in 1876 to meet their death at the Little Big Horn, the Seventh Cavalry Band played "The Girl I Left Behind

Me," while Army wives and their children waved farewell.

The Sixth Infantry made an excellent impression when it marched because of the lively flourish of its music and especially because of the commanding presence of its drum major. Sgt. "Slim" Chapman, six feet four inches tall, towered over the others and led them through their intricate maneuvers on the parade ground. The Band was the center of the Friday afternoon reviews and played concerts on Sundays and holidays in the bandstand in front of the Officers' Club. It was also an important part of the celebration on Memorial Day, when people flocked out from St. Louis to honor the dead in the Post Cemetery, and on Regimental Day, when the Sixth Infantry would review its past accomplishments and take cognizance of its present potential.

While my father had his routine, my mother also had hers. First of all, it was keeping the house clean and herself and her children clothed and fed. Keeping growing children clothed on the little money available was a problem, but in one way or another the Army helped. The men could draw any number of things for their families—beds, bedding, furniture. They could draw Army blankets, which often ended up on the backs of their offspring. They could also draw as much woolen underwear as they wanted, and so most of them would, like my father, draw enough extra underwear for their children. My mother would cut it down, and although it scratched, it got us through the winter. Inett Layton, the daughter of Sgt. Boyd Layton, the Mess Sergeant of Service Company, and my constant companion, recalls that for young girls the annual routine went like this: "At Easter woolen underwear came off, and patent leather shoes and whoopie socks went on."

Winter underwear came whole, but summer underwear was another thing. Sergeant Layton would bring home the flour sacks from his mess, and my mother would bleach them to remove the labels and make them into B.V.D.s for his children and hers. My mother's sewing prowess became well known, and she soon found herself employed by friends and neighbors, and finally, of course, by the officers' wives. From the time we moved onto the post, dressmaking occupied a great part of her time. The hum of my mother's sewing machine accompanied the trill of my father's clarinet on evenings when the only sounds outside were the hoot of the owls in the big oaks or taps echoing through the woods. Some of the officers' wives were not exactly beautifully proportioned. The uglier they were—the more big-hipped and sway-backed—the more impossible seemed their demands. They would arrive with a flowery bundle of stuff draped over one arm, a dress or an outfit to be made over. And my mother somehow accepted them all, no matter how impossible their requests. For remaking any sort of frock, which frequently amounted to a virtual miracle, she charged $2.50, which the ladies often paid under protest. To make a plain cotton dress, for which she would often draw the pattern herself, she charged only fifty cents. Her dressmaking turned our little house into a place of magic, the swatches of bright material whisked through the air like bright tropical birds, suddenly all brought to rest each in its proper place. And no matter how little money there was, she seemed always to be able to whip up something for herself that had just the right shape and color and was the envy of her less imaginative neighbors.

My mother also began to serve at officers' tea parties and luncheons, mainly in the quarters of lieutenants and captains. The officers of higher rank usually had help in the house—often Filipino servants whom they had brought back from the Orient. These men did the cooking, cleaning, and baby-sitting and took complete care of the house. When no Filipinos were available, the colonel or major simply assigned an enlisted man to come to clean, cook, baby-sit, and serve as his chauffeur as well. These "dog-robbers" were usually young Pfc's who had no objection because this assignment meant that they would be excused from drill and from other duties.

At Jefferson Barracks, as on the frontier garrisons of the past, it was the old story of Mrs. O'Grady and the colonel's lady. In this case it was Mrs. Murphy, the wife of a civilian employee on the post who lived near the North Gate, who was called upon to cook for large parties at the Officers' Club, where the bachelor officers lived, or at the houses of the colonel or lieutenant colonel. It was Mrs. Murphy who first enlisted my mother to help her serve. From then on she would put on a white nurse's uniform that had been provided for her and would serve at a party for twenty people or more. The nature of these gatherings may be glimpsed from references to them in the issues of the Sunday St. Louis *Post-Dispatch*, where some of the Jefferson Barracks society notes of January 1931 read like a court circular:

> Colonel and Mrs. Pegram Whitworth entertained the officers and women of the garrison with an informal reception on New Year's Day.

> Major and Mrs. Arthur Underwood entertained at dinner before the New Year's Eve hop.

The Post Bridge Club held a bi-monthly
meeting at the Officers Club Monday
evening with Major and Mrs. Arnold
Reeve, Captain and Mrs. Raymond I.
Lovell, Captain and Mrs. Clifford D. Over-
felt and Mrs. Joseph Catte as the hosts and
hostesses.

Sometimes for a dinner party my mother would
take me with her, and I would rest on a sofa on the
screened-in porch while dinner was served inside.
Since almost all the officers had been overseas, their
houses were rich in wicker and mahogany furniture.
Huge brass trays shone like full moons against the
dark tables. I would fix my eyes on their bright sur-
faces and think of the miles and miles of ocean that
had brought them here. The gold would slowly sink
into the rising waves, the bugle would echo faintly
through the dark, and I would fall asleep.

6

THE WESTERN FRONT

While everything on the garrison was regimented, there were always a few buildings off to the side near the woods that did not fit into the general plan of things and where life went on in a disorganized way, as it did on small farms in the neighboring area. Here, occasionally, you could see an automobile tire attached to the branch of an oak tree to serve as a child's swing, and a child swinging in it out over a sinkhole. A group of brick quarters for enlisted men situated on low ground behind the barracks surrounding the parade ground was always referred to as the "Battle Ship." The long cantonment buildings on the western side of the post constituted what was known as the "Western Front." The buildings were divided so that four or five families occupied each one. We lived in the topmost one, diagonally across from the K.C. Building, for a two-year period when my father was a sergeant.

Thrown up quickly to serve as barracks during World War I, the buildings had once been neat and symmetrical, but they now appeared worn away as if their white paint had been attacked by blight. The buildings were parallel to one another, and the ground on which they rested sloped to a steam plant at the bottom, which provided steam for the barracks. This particular bottom area was later christened, during World War II, "Pneumonia Gulch." Because of the slope of the land, in some cases there was a long flight of steps at the front of a building while the back rested on ground level. The unevenness of the steps made them all look like houses constructed by children from mechanical toys. Along the buildings was a strange assortment of screened-in porches, all somewhat askew, many enclosed in morning-glory vines in the summer. In front of each were flowers—roses, nasturtiums, marigolds, beds of canna, with sunflowers along the back fences. In their asymmetry and with the thick growth of summer vegetation, they resembled barges blown there in a hurricane, abandoned and overgrown.

A sidewalk ran down the hill in front of the buildings, and in an open field at the bottom, just before the steam plant and opposite the Chapel, was a row of sandbagged trenches, which from the time of World War I had been used for bayonet drill. The sandbags were soggy and split open, and the gunny sacks containing them were wet and falling apart. The trenches always had a terrible dankness and an unmistakable smell of decay. The stuffed straw figures that served as targets for the bayonet course were straight out of a terrifying fairy tale.

The bayonet course was a constant reminder of the serious business for which our fathers were preparing; another, although I was unable to read it fully at the time, was the coat of arms of the Sixth Infantry, which my father wore on his lapel button. The same coat of arms, painted in bright colors, covered the entire south wall of the gymnasium in Atkinson Hall, where basketball games and regimental balls were held. The crest consisted of a red lion's face on a wreath of the colors of the regiment, silver and red, and represented the service of the Sixth Infantry in the campaigns in Canada in 1813 and 1814. The shield was white, the color of infantry facings on the uniforms in 1812, the year the regiment was organized. At the top of the shield was a silver cross on a red field, the coat of arms of the ancient Lords of Dun (it was near the city of Dun that the Sixth Infantry crossed the Meuse River in World War I). At the bottom was the motto "Unity is Strength" in green letters on a silver scroll. But it was the central part of the shield that always fascinated me and whose significance I did not then understand.

Centered on the shield was a green alligator, and below it, a green scaling ladder. At maneuvers held at Camp Custer, near Battle Creek, Michigan, in July 1934 a fight broke out between the men of the Sixth Infantry and those of the Second Infantry, when a man of the Second, in the course of a friendly argument, made the mistake of attacking the Sixth's central emblem. The men of the Sixth Infantry were so low-down, he commented, that they had to climb a ladder "to kiss an alligator's ass." After the riot that followed, the Second Infantry was moved to the other end of the bivouac area.

The alligator symbolized the heroic service of the Sixth Infantry in the Seminole War of 1837, and the green ladder the storming of the citadel of Chapultepec in 1847; the green was the green of Mexico. The Seminole War, which began in 1835 and lasted for nearly eight years, was the most costly Indian war in which the United States engaged. A large part of the Seminole tribe, an offshoot of the Creeks and the Choctaws, refused to accept the Treaty of Paynes Landing in 1832 and move west of the Mississippi. Led by Osceola, they held out in the Everglades, and even when the war was concluded, some still resisted; they remain there today, a reminder of the first war that the United States failed to win. One of the bloodiest engagements of this war was the Battle of Okeechobee Swamp on Christmas Day, 1837. Colonel Gentry, the leader of a regiment of 600 volunteers from Missouri, was killed early in the battle, and the brunt of the fighting was borne by the men of the Sixth Infantry. Seventy-five percent of the men of the seven companies participating were either killed or wounded, and in one company only four men remained uninjured. With a single exception, every officer was wounded. Col. Abner R. Thompson, although wounded three times, his head held above the swamp water, gave his last command, which became the motto of the regiment, "Keep steady, men. Charge the hummock, and remember the regiment to which you belong." Charge the hummock, indeed! The picture of scores of wounded men slogging their way through the swamp to reach a hummock only a few feet above water is not a pretty one. It is understandable that the Battle of Okeechobee Swamp went down in history as "Bloody Christmas."

While their lapel buttons reminded the men of the past glories of their regiment, reminders of other aspects of Army life were also very much in evidence. The guardhouse at the center of the parade ground alerted the men to what happened to those who failed to follow the rules. It was distinguished from the other buildings by being square and one-story, surrounded by a broad open porch in ironic contrast to the cell-block it contained. On this porch, guard details assembled. The guardhouse was known as Claytor's Hotel, after the provost sergeant in charge, Oscar Claytor. Sergeant Claytor wore an officer's stripe on the sleeve of his uniform, indicating that he had been an officer in World War I. Many jokes went the rounds of the Barracks about Claytor's obesity. A guard in one of the companies is supposed to have reported one day that someone had pitched a huge tent on the parade ground. On close inspection, the tent proved to be Oscar Claytor in his sun tans. But there was no joke about the severity of the treatment the men received at Claytor's hand.

Guarding the prisoners on their ordinary rounds —picking up the garbage, trimming the lawns, washing the windows—was the duty of regular soldiers. "Chasing prisoners" was a job the men hated. The guard had to follow each pair with his rifle at the ready. The prisoners, dressed in dark blue fatigue clothes, bore on their backs either a white star if they had a light sentence and were trustees or a red star if their sentence was more severe. The fatigue clothes themselves, which all the enlisted men wore for heavy work, had a ludicrous quality to their shapelessness. With their floppy matching hats and sacklike cut, they seemed designed more for a crew of circus clowns than for serious workmen. They deprived the prisoner of any claim to individual dignity. Like prison garb in a comic strip they turned their wearer, whatever his physical or mental dimensions, into a pathetic wasted figure, a walking scarecrow.

Prisoners were very much a part of garrison life. A pair would be seen policing the grounds, picking up scraps of paper, or pulling out weeds from between the stones of the gutters, stones taken from the original limestone buildings of the garrison when they had been demolished, while boys nearby played softball or a family picnicked under a tree. But the prisoners did sometimes escape, and it was terrifying to try to sleep in a flimsy beaver-boarded room while the bugle sounded through the lonely hills and even the tapping of branches on the window took on the magnified sound of drum beats in the dark. Armed with a meat cleaver, a certain Kosko once managed to make his way into the woods, and every inch of the entire reservation was soon being combed by squads of armed men in search of him. They never found him; he threaded his way back through their traps and turned himself in days later at the guardhouse.

The escaped prisoner, if he was hiding, would no doubt be in one of the sinkholes, which were, at the best of times, frightening. Sinkholes were very much a part of the terrain, and how they came about nobody seems quite sure. Their existence has sometimes been attributed to the 1811 earthquake along the New Madrid, Missouri, fault. The effects of this earthquake had been extraordinarily severe: the Mississippi had changed its course, and part of it was left behind to form Real Foot Lake in Tennessee. The limestone in Missouri, which is highly cavernous, may simply have

given way on this or on other occasions when water
infiltrated it and have sunk into inverted cones. At the
bottom tip of each cone a rock-covered hole filled with
water led to an underground stream. In time, vegetation—brambles and vines—covered the hole. It was
like approaching the entrance to the underworld
when, as children, we ventured through the vines
down to the edge of the pit.

A Battle of the Sinkhole took place near Fort
Howard, Wisconsin, in 1815 when a band of Indians
took refuge in a sinkhole near the fort, and a bloody
battle ensued. Capt. Albert Tracy, stationed at Jefferson Barracks during the Civil War, tells in his journal
of seeing a light one evening and of setting out to
investigate: "It was very dark generally, and the sinkholes, or pits, in our path difficult to be wholly avoided.
It was so late, too, being past midnight, that every
sound except perhaps the cry of the wild-cats, or the
owls across the river, was wholly hushed." He and the
sergeant with him waded through the tall, wet grass
and finally found that the light was coming from a fire
in the brush. Two men, one a recruit who had earlier
abandoned his post, were roasting chickens they had
picked up from one of the henroosts in the neighborhood. For this infraction, one of the men was punished
by a ride on the wooden horse—sitting for some time
astride a horizontal pole raised to a height of eight or
nine feet—and the other man was turned over for trial
by civil authorities and then given a dishonorable
discharge.

The order book kept at Jefferson Barracks in 1843
by Stephen Watts Kearny, then a colonel commanding
the Third Military Department (most of the Great
Plains region), lists a number of dishonorable dis-
charges. A certain Pvt. Patrick McIntyre was charged

with "(1) conduct subversive of good order and military discipline, (2) drunkenness, and (3) utter worthlessness." He had said to a guard on duty, "You are a son of a bitch," or something to that effect. He was found guilty of all three charges, except that the word "utter" was deleted in the third charge, and he was drummed out of the service.

At the turn of the century the Army enlisted man in the United States was treated as an outcast, a worthless individual. Soldiers were not allowed to enter respectable places of entertainment, and respectable young women would never be seen with them in public. The number of desertions during the fiscal year ending June 1889 had increased at such an alarming rate that something clearly had to be done. To investigate the situation Frank L. Woodward of the St. Louis *Post-Dispatch* enlisted at Jefferson Barracks, and in a series of articles, collected in *The Dogs of War* (1890), he made some sensational charges. The officers of the post, he said, were unnecessarily cruel and overbearing; the food was unfit to eat; vermin infested the quarters; and men were placed under arrest on the most trivial charges and confined to the guardhouse, which was indescribably filthy. President Harrison set up a board of inquiry, conditions at the Barracks improved greatly, and the number of desertions diminished.

One reason for the increased desertions at the turn of the century was the good economic condition of the country; life outside the Army was better than life within. In the twenties and thirties the opposite was the case: because of the Great Depression, the Army attracted many men it might not have drawn in better periods. Fewer men went over the hill, but the prisoners were a reminder that there were still those who did not observe the discipline required. Those who broke the rules were known as "Bolsheviks," and they inevitably ended up in the guardhouse. The children of the garrison were held as fully accountable as their fathers for not behaving in a seemly fashion. When on the school bus one afternoon several tough sons of enlisted men placed a condom in the pocketbook of the plump teen-age daughter of the battalion commander, they were hauled before him at Headquarters, as on another occasion was a group of boys caught swimming in the post watertank. Along with their fathers, they were made to realize that such actions would not be tolerated.

Most of the time life on the Western Front went by calmly without anything at all happening. In our quarters we had acquired two items that demonstrated the temporary betterment of my father's position—an old upright piano and a telephone. The telephone was a positive link with my classmates in South St. Louis, and on the piano my mother played by ear a number of lovely old songs and I spent long hours picking out scales and trying to read music. Outside, with my companions, I used the sandbagged trenches of the bayonet course with their straw figures as a playground, never thinking of the purpose for which they had been designed, although I never liked their dankness and smell of decay.

7

THE BOOTLEG BUSINESS

How it was that we entered what my father called the "Bootleg Business" I am not quite sure. But it began with our moving in the spring of 1930 from the Barracks to what was known as the Boston house. A sergeant named Boston, who had retired to St. Augustine, Florida, to manage a national cemetery, owned the sizeable two-story square frame structure which looked out on the North Gate entrance to Jefferson Barracks. The address, 9988 South Broadway, indicated that it was indeed the last house.

The North Gate, the main gate to the Barracks, consisted of two large gate posts made of square white limestone blocks topped with black-painted cannon balls. Next to the gate posts was the sentry box, where the guard on duty stopped each car as it approached the gate to inquire about the purpose of its visit, its destination, and then, usually without further ado, to wave it past. Although cars were rarely turned away, the guard made clear to each driver that he was entering a special domain. Even the Dinky or Toonerville

Trolley, whose tracks into the Barracks curved past the North Gate opposite the Boston house, had to stop long enough for the guard to make sure that all was right on board before it could proceed.

We had been threatened for some time with having to move. Each time there was a post-wide inspection by the commanding officer or by an area commander, word would get out that the unsightly cantonment buildings were to be torn down. They were eyesores. But usually there would be a year's reprieve—until the next major white-glove inspection. But finally the ax fell, and we were told that we would have to move. Our next-door neighbors for several years on the Western Front had been Sergeant and Mrs. O'Hara and their three children, Billy, Marie, and Colleen. They were now our closest friends, and we did not want to lose touch with them. As Sergeant O'Hara had only two more years of service before retiring, he did not want to settle in any permanent way in the county. It was decided that we would occupy the Boston house together, the O'Haras in the three ground-floor rooms and we in the three upstairs rooms, all sharing the one bathroom on the second floor.

The front hallway was papered in a dark flowery paper, and the stairs led up to our living room, furnished with a fake leather divanet and a wicker chaise longue belonging to the O'Haras, who had spent some years in the Philippines and had many mementos to show for it. They did not have room for the chaise longue in their cramped quarters downstairs, and it became for me the most important and exotic piece that the house possessed. It had pockets on each side, and it seemed the height of luxury to be able to put up my feet and stretch out with books at my elbows and to imagine the gentle movement of palm fronds overhead; it was here that I wrote my first poems. The two books that I kept in the pockets of the chaise longue I had discovered in the Bostons' basement storeroom, *Poems of the Great War*, edited by J.W. Cunliffe, and *One Hundred and One Famous Poems*, compiled by Roy J. Cook. In the latter I discovered Wordsworth's "Ode: Intimations of Immortality," which became one of my favorites, and although I could not fully understand the meaning of the lines, I read them over and over:

> Though nothing can bring back the hour
> Of splendor in the grass, of glory in the flower:
> We will grieve not, rather find
> Strength in what remains behind ...

Off our living room was the kitchen, which had a metal sink and a window looking out over the backyard. The front bedroom had windows right above the street, which opened on a large oak tree. Through the branches the lights of the sentry box at the gate shone all during the night. Because the ground fell away steeply from the street, the Boston house appeared to be perched on a high hill. A driveway led down beside the house, on the reservation side, to a garage at the bottom. In a corner next to it was an old outhouse, the remnant of an earlier era. A long back porch ran the length of the house, and stairs from it led up to our kitchen. In the middle of the backyard was a broken-down grape arbor.

The backyard did not look very promising when we first arrived; the previous tenants had left tin cans and rubbish everywhere. Within a short time, as self-appointed gardener, I would have the yard cleaned up with shovel and rake. Down in one corner was an open level spot which I would turn annually into a garden. While I began by planting several different kinds of vegetables, I settled in the end on string beans as being the easiest and really the most satisfying. I delighted in turning over the rich loam in the spring, putting in the seeds, and then watching the beans sprout and soon leap round their poles. In the summer heat there was a whole world of looping and tangled vines producing long, luscious beans.

On one side of the house were pear and cherry trees and a great clump of mock orange in one corner. There were lilacs in profusion right off the back porch and violets in clumps in the spring. We shared with the O'Haras the entire expense of the house, the rent of which was thirty dollars a month.

In the fall of 1931, after we had occupied the Boston house for more than a year, I began Cleveland High School in St. Louis, and soon afterward the O'Haras departed for Long Beach, California. Just as there was a rigid order to life on the reservation, so there was also a precise order to the retirement of both enlisted men and officers. There were certain enclaves in Florida and California to which they gravitated then as now. For years I had heard talk of Long Beach with its mild climate and sunshine as an ideal haven for retired enlisted men. The O'Haras packed up their car and were off, like many of their breed before them, to Long Beach, and we were faced with the difficult problem of having to move again.

My parents talked first of sharing the house with another couple in the Band, but my father opposed this. The O'Haras had to leave a number of pieces of furniture behind—an electric refrigerator (a Kelvinator, one of the early models) and a complete dining room outfit. My mother spent days making dresses for the O'Hara girls to pay for them.

My father then came up with the proposal that we

go into the "Bootleg Business" and take over the entire house. His idea was to make some home brew and invite his fellow Bandsmen from the Barracks to share it with him and thus make a small profit which would take care of our increased rent and give us an easy and comfortable place to live in. My mother was not exactly enchanted by the plan, especially since she did not drink herself, but she did not oppose it on moral grounds. She was quite aware that there were bootleg joints all over St. Louis County and that most of them were frequented by my father. If the police cared that the law was being broken, they never gave any indication of it. As long as the establishments were quiet, they didn't object. And the Army itself would be the last to object. The bootlegger was after all only offering a needed service. There were so many bootleggers in Lemay that it was said that you could fall off one porch and onto another and never miss a round of drinks. A man named Singer ran a bootleg joint down the street from us in a large white frame house. He had been in business for years and raked in the money from his military customers. His place was their first stop off the base. My mother's frugal nature may have been attracted by the notion that some of my father's meager salary would not be going into some-one else's pockets.

Liquor had always been available in one way or another on the post. When the regular ration of early days was discontinued, whiskey was provided by the sutler who ran the garrison's general store. When the sutler in turn was forbidden to sell spirits, the men would exchange provisions purchased from him for spirits obtained from civilians. My father was not the first enlisted man to engage in the production of home brew. Sergeant Daley, who produced home brew and wine, made the mistake of selling it at the rifle range at Arcadia and was caught. Sergeant Ailsworth, whose wife "Madam Queen" became celebrated throughout the garrison for her bright curly hennaed hair, had taken his own supply of home brew in a hay wagon and had hidden it at one point in the ammunition dump of a sinkhole to avoid detection.

My father may have been prompted in his decision to make his own beer by an article that appeared in the January 24, 1932, issue of the St. Louis *Post-Dispatch*. G.K. Chesterton, who was to speak a few days later at the Odeon Theater on "Culture and the Coming Peril," had this to say: "In one of the weekly articles I sent home, I suggested that we prohibit everything. It appears that if we can keep prohibition a while we may have a real revival of the ancient art of home brewing. It's merely a matter of time until everyone does it, and does it well. The devil, as usual working against his will, the will of God seems to be on the point of restoring some of the old arts of the household. Let the Government only prohibit everything — boots, shoes, coats, hats, tables, chairs — on high moral grounds, and man will once again start doing the old domestic crafts, to the vast increase of his intelligence and peace of mind."

The Noble Experiment was on its way out. The Wickersham Law Enforcement Commission had announced a few days before Chesterton's visit that it felt that it was impossible to ban beer and wine in homes. The report of the Commission had said: "Why home wine making should be lawful while home brewing of beer and home distilling of spirits are not; why home wine making for home use is less reprehensible than making the same wine outside the home for home use, and why it should be penal to make wine commercially for use in home and not penal to make in huge quantities the material for wine making and set up an elaborate selling campaign for disposing of them is not apparent." The report lashed out at the failure of prohibition forces to entrap the real leaders of the bootlegging business. "In place of the small still operated by the individual moonshiner, there are plants of a capacity fairly comparable to the old-time lawful distillery.... The business of maintaining and operating them is well-organized." Mindful that most operators, big or small, would not be harassed, we began. Probably from Singer or other bootlegging associates my father acquired all the equipment necessary for the business, a ten-gallon stone crock and several cases of bottles, and soon the first batch of home brew was ready for consumption.

The procedure for making it was simple. Two large cans of malt were needed for the ten-gallon crock. The cans of malt with their yellow labels—resembling yellow cans of Mexican tamales but bigger and fatter—covered with reproductions of medals won at various fairs and expositions had an appropriate plump German appearance. Water was heated on the gas range in the kitchen in a large kettle and the two cans of malt were stirred in. When the mixture cooled and yeast had been added, it was taken to the cellar and poured into the crock, which was then covered over with cheese cloth and tied with a string to keep out gnats and bugs. The mixture was left overnight, and the next day a large Irish potato was cut into three pieces and tossed into the crock. The starch in the potato pieces would cause the yeast to settle to the bottom.

Although it was advisable to wait longer, our brew was ready for bottling in two or three days. A short piece of hose was dropped into the crock and the brew siphoned out into bottles that contained a small amount of sugar. You had to be careful not to drop the hose down too close to the bottom so as not to get the yeast all stirred up. Then you would draw in on the hose to get the brew started. Since Richie and I were designated to help with the bottling, we also had to siphon off the stuff to get it started. While I now think that there is nothing more refreshing than good cold beer, I then found the taste or even the smell of my father's abhorrent. I recall it as having the smell of old wet Army shoes and the taste of a soggy blanket.

When the bottles were filled, each one was set under the simple capper that brought down the cap on the bottle, sealing it airtight, and that was that. The bottles were put in cases, the cases stacked up, and the brew was ready for drinking.

The home brew was deposited in the Kelvinator in the kitchen, and it did not stay there long. The men on the post were ready to drink anything they could find. Soon there were any number of thirsty Bandsmen gathered around our dining table. The beer was priced at ten cents a pint. It was sometimes bottled in quart bottles and sold by the glass, at five cents a glass. Before long, men from all the other companies were arriving every evening, and, considering the amount of brew consumed, there should have been a profit. But from the beginning my father made the mistake of giving credit. He was forced to do so because most of the men had no cash whatever during the month: it all came on payday and disappeared at once. My father kept track of the glasses consumed by making marks on a pad, and then on payday the men were supposed to come in and pay up. There were fewer poker games on the post in those days than there had been when the

Sixth Infantry had first arrived and the men had saved up their money on the march across the country. But most of them were making a mere pittance anyway, and some of them were married. There was little money left to spend on drink.

Some of the men came regularly and paid up. There was Beerbaum, a thin blond horn player, a graduate of the University of Illinois. We were, of course, at the height of the Great Depression, and many of the men had turned to the military when there was no place else to turn. There was another college graduate, a full-blooded Indian, six feet four inches tall, "Big Ike," a Sioux, the star of the Band's basketball team. The men called him "Chief." He was a gentle, kind man, who from time to time brought his tall blonde wife, just as blonde as he was dark. She had a job in North St. Louis, and they came together usually only on weekends. Another Indian member of the Band and also a steady customer was "Little Ike," a Comanche. A Polish-American clarinetist named Trask sometimes brought his very attractive Polish girlfriend. Another young clarinetist from southern Illinois, Clyde Maynard, brought his pretty young wife Louise. She did not like Army life at all, and soon managed to persuade her husband to give it up. She and Clyde, who both were favorites of my mother's, became her life-long friends, and mine as well.

Although there were in general few women customers, there was one regular one—Adele Grimble, the wife of Sergeant Grimble. The Grimbles had been our next-door neighbors in the K.C. Building on the post, and now lived around the corner on Teddy Avenue. Dell Grimble had served for years as secretary to the supply officer of the post, and her husband was a barber. Together they knew all the gossip. Dell

Grimble, a plumpish little woman with delicate, doll-like features and a quick laugh, was a descendant of the original settlers of Carondelet who had deeded the land of the Barracks to the Army in 1826. She naturally took a proprietary interest in the reservation, and was a mine of information about it. Her mother, the wife of Pvt. "Pop" Stewart, who operated the hog ranch on the post, still spoke the French that her family had always spoken. I began to take weekly lessons with her when I was only eight or nine, and by the time I came to study French in high school, I already had a certain proficiency in the language. Mrs. Stewart was to me a grand old lady, and living as she did in a little house tucked away in the woods as in a fairy tale, it seemed to me absolutely natural that she should speak another language.

Most of our bootlegging customers were loners— men like Holbrook, the snare drummer, a small man with a shriveled-up face. Or Sgt. "Cat" Collins of Service Company, a solid, red-faced, square-shouldered man in his fifties who had served in Panama and elsewhere overseas, an old-timer who had no end of stories to tell. "Cat" Collins took the part of Santa Claus every Christmas Eve in the Post Chapel. Then there was Upchurch, perhaps the steadiest customer. He was an emaciated, gray-haired wisp of a man with black horn-rimmed glasses and a roll-your-own, Bull Durham cigarette constantly dangling from his mouth. As prim and precise as a country school teacher, he took down the orders at the Commissary on regular printed forms.

"Nothing," Upchurch said emphatically, when he heard that I was interested in poetry, "is poetry if it does not rhyme." I knew perfectly well that there were many poems that did not rhyme, but I realized that it was hopeless to discuss the subject with Up-church. His statement simply reinforced my basic distrust of him.

Upchurch became a permanent fixture, and his consumption of home brew did nothing to fatten him up, but he went on consuming it all the same. He would run up a bill of $100 or more and still be there every evening soon after retreat. He was deeply in debt to us when we closed down our bootlegging operation years later.

The greatest propriety was always observed. My mother did not drink at all, and she sat down with the men as if she had been receiving them in her parlor down South.

During the week no session in the evening lasted very late: most of the men had to be back on the post and in their bunks in time for reveille at 5:30 the next morning. That usually meant that, not having money for carfare, they would have to walk back the mile through the woods. My father had to be up and off at seven in the morning. The big gatherings took place on weekends, especially after payday. Because the men just came and stayed, my mother was persuaded to provide them with food. She cooked huge meals— baked ham, fried chicken, and turkey, with cornbread and her own hot rolls. A delicious dinner with all the fixings was priced at only fifty cents. The men were delighted to have all the benefits of home—and home as many of them had never known it—for so little.

It became clear as time went by that home brew and food were not bringing in much money. And so my father decided to begin dealing in hard liquor. A dark good-looking young man soon pulled up and parked his elegant black coupé in front of our house and brought from it a rectangular leather case, which

78

he carried to the back of the house and up the long steps to our kitchen. His leather case, which he then opened, fitted neatly around a five-gallon can of pure alcohol. It was probably through old experienced bootlegging hands like Singer, whose customers all paid cash, that my father had found out how to get in touch with the charming, polite young man who also brought to our kitchen an oak barrel and cases of whiskey bottles, pints and half-pints. The oak barrel was soon installed on its side in a frame on the shelf of the closet in the middle room upstairs, which was the bedroom that Richie and I shared. My father would cut the alcohol in half, adding five gallons of water to five gallons of alcohol. This mixture was poured into the oak barrel, whose charcoal-lined interior would color the alcohol in due time. To speed up the process my father tried first putting prunes into the barrel, but the prunes gave the liquor a bitter taste. He again consulted the experts, and the gentleman caller brought, along with his next leather-encased delivery, an electric needle about six inches long. It was a steel rod like a soldering iron. The needle would be plugged in, and, when red, would be inserted in the hole in the barrel and remain there for two or three days. The alcohol would then absorb the flavor and the coloring from the barrel. And the whiskey, selling for forty cents a half-pint and seventy-five cents a pint, was as fine as any that could be acquired in the county. At least it was cut in a clean and decent way, and in those days that was just about all that anyone could ask.

In the process of the "cutting," the alcoholic vapors that emerged from my closet made me feel when I went to bed that I was about to be hauled off to an operating room. The room had been intended as a kitchen, and the large gunmetal gray sink that greeted me when I awoke gave me the sensation of being locked up in some evil and foul-smelling laboratory.

The alcoholic vapors that swept my room haunted me even when I left the house. I began to think of the entire business as not only extremely distasteful but also dangerously unlawful. At first, involved with my own activities at school, I had thought little about the business and even welcomed the visitors it brought to our house, which had previously had so few guests. In the early stages everything was discreet: only a hand-ful of men came to the house, and they usually arrived after dark. Now that we sold hard liquor as well as home brew, a steady stream of men would dart in and out, especially on payday, just to pick up a bottle—right under the nose of the guard at the gate.

I now realize that the guard could probably not have cared less, even if brawls had taken place and men had been tossed out in front of him on the pave-ment. All this was not his concern: he was there to check the cars coming in and out of the Barracks. But then he seemed to me—as indeed he was—the symbol of authority, an authority which one day was sure to crack down on us. Our house was so close to the gate that from the windows of the front bedroom I could gaze down through the branches of the oak tree in our front yard right onto the gate. I could hear every word that the guard said and could almost make out what he was writing down on his pad. The lights of the passing cars, reflected upward, threw the oak branches into grotesque relief on the ceiling. The front bed-room was the one farthest from the noise of the drinkers down below, and I would frequently repair to it in the evening. Whenever a car drew up and parked in front of the house or across the street for any length of time, I would hold my breath: this was surely a private detective who was waiting for the police to

80

arrive. The siren would sound momentarily, a police car would wheel in, making a U-turn and discharging its burly occupants right on our front steps. Then there would be a banging on the front door—I could hear it down below right then—and we would all be whisked off, hands high in the air, tears streaming down my mother's face, to spend years in jail. The scene that I pictured while the great beaked shadows came and went on the bedroom ceiling was straight out of one of the films that I had seen at the post picture show. The bootleggers in the films all traveled in big cars in big cities—but we were allied to them, I thought, and our alliance could only bring us to a bad end.

If the evenings made me apprehensive, the days were in their own way just as terrifying. A large World War I liberty truck picked up the Army children of the neighborhood to take them to school in the morning and bring them back in the afternoon. Our school bus had none of the amenities of the modern yellow pumpkin coach. Covered with heavy khaki canvas held hooped over us, it had no windows and three long benches, one on each side and one down the middle, along which we squeezed like so many lumps of dough or squirming fish. To help us on and off and to watch over us, we had a "bus sergeant." He was not a sergeant, but a private detailed for this not exactly delectable duty. The Barracks bus made several stops, first at Hancock School on South Broadway, then at Carondelet and Blow Elementary Schools in Carondelet, and then farther up in South St. Louis at Cleveland High School. Our front porch was the gathering place each morning for the children of the neighborhood. Our parlor and dining room were still heavy with the smell of home brew and tobacco from the night before, and I lived in terror that one of my schoolmates would burst into the house one morning, discover a mass of empty beer glasses on the table or in the sink, and find us out. I hated the school bus anyway; its high metal gate pinned us in like animals, and like animals we behaved. Children can be cruel to one another, even under the best of circumstances, but caged up as we were, the brute element predominated.

In reality no one said anything to me directly about our bootlegging, but I found intimations of what many of them knew in much of what they said. In dreams at night I would hear the kids all singing:

> We're going on a picnic,
> Who will be there?

> George

> Cecile

> Inett

> Luther

> Tommy...

In my dream I would call out the names of all my companions on the school bus, and then their song would conclude as all their fingers pointed to me:

> I'll bring the sandwiches
> And *you* bring the beer...

I would awake in a cold sweat and listen while in the still night a car would pull up at the North Gate, pause for a moment that seemed an eternity, and then continue on, its sound trailing off as it wound around the sinkholes toward the heart of the Barracks.

8

THE EXPRESSION TEACHER

My anxiety about the evils of bootlegging was fortunately relieved at this time by the sudden appearance in my life of a magical personage. While we still lived on the post, there appeared one day at our door on the Western Front a woman in black silk with a sparkling pin on her enormous bosom and a large floppy black straw hat. She propelled herself into the room on the thinnest high heels that I had ever seen. Massive, erect, indomitable, she came forward into our small house like the great prow of a ship. Her speech, which seemed more song than speech because of the full timbre of her voice, was like fireworks, and it came forth in a steady stream. I had long been accustomed to talk: in my Southern family, I had been surrounded by people who never stopped talking. But I had never met anyone who spoke like this. She used words that I had seen only on the pages of books, and she spoke them as I had dreamed they would be spoken. And what she offered was the entrance to a magic world. She was quite simply a witch, a good

83

fairy, who had appeared at just the right time.

She was a voice teacher, and the means that she offered to sweep me off to her magic realm was the marvelous instrument of the human voice. This was Mrs. Emma Nettie Bradbury, whose husband, a surgeon at the Veterans Administration Hospital adjoining the Barracks, had recently died. She had studied speech at the University of Chicago and had given readings of poetry and plays at ladies' clubs in St. Louis. She came now to make the rounds of the houses of enlisted men and officers at the Barracks to line up students for classes in elocution—or "expression," as she was careful to call it—at the Post Chapel. I was one of the first to enroll, and when the others, older and younger, dropped by the wayside and Mrs. Bradbury no longer came out to the post, I was the only one who remained with her, joining her other pupils regularly in her home in South St. Louis.

No sooner had I enrolled than Mrs. Bradbury decided that I was to be the star of her troupe. She would prepare me for the stage, and I would become a great actor through the cultivation of my voice. My voice was then changing, but Mrs. Bradbury contended that there was no need for it to change in the usual raucous cracking way but simply through proper exercise it would evolve into the full rich baritone that would bring me fame and fortune. Mrs. Bradbury spoke of the diaphragm as the mysterious golden key, whose proper use could make all the difference to the actor and the singer. I had never even heard of the diaphragm, had no idea where or what it was, and had certainly not been instructed in its use. But I began to see that there was indeed a difference between those who spoke from the throat straining their vocal chords, and those who spoke—as God intended them to speak and as all Mrs. Bradbury's pupils were certainly going to speak—*from* the diaphragm.

I would stand in my bedroom, while the vapors drifted from my closet, and practice by the hour the exercises that she gave me, modulating carefully each vowel sound. I stood—as she taught me to stand—on the balls of my feet, ready to shift the weight from one to the other and to enter when my cue came to deliver my magnificent lines. Or else I sat reading over and over to myself a passage of poetry she had given me to memorize and which she had carefully marked to indicate the inflections of the voice, the pauses, and the stresses:

> If music be the food of love, play on;
> Give me excess of it, that, surfeiting,
> The appetite may sicken, and so die.
> That strain again! it had a dying fall:
> O, it came o'er my ear like the sweet sound,
> That breathes upon a bank of violets,
> Stealing and giving odor! . . .

I was soon drunk not on the alcoholic vapors that I was breathing in but on poetry. I had fallen in love totally, blissfully, and eternally with language.

As I became more and more involved with Mrs. Bradbury's studio and took part in her recitals and theatricals, the Bootleg Business, while still very much around me, receded quietly into the background. Mrs. Bradbury called her establishment the Nautilus Studio: it was to grow like the nautilus ("Build thee more stately mansions, O my soul"—as Oliver Wendell Holmes had said in his poem "The Chambered Nautilus," from which she took the name) and as each of her pupils would grow.

Who are we? Who are we?
We're the pupils of Mrs. B.
What do we like? What do we like?
We like knowledge that makes us bright,

we sang in unison. I became one of the Nautilus Players, performing Shakespeare and George Bernard
Shaw, and won the first Bradbury medal for reading.

Some of the exercises Mrs. Bradbury gave me were
strange, but I carefully went through them all the
same. Once—for what reason I do not recall, but for
concentration I suppose—I was told to sit as long as
possible, holding an alarm clock on my lap, and just
to watch the hands go round, and I did. While there
were many voice exercises, there were also exercises in
diction and vocabulary. There were other exercises in
cultural background, lists of operas with their char-
acters, and synopses of Shakespeare's plays. Mrs.
Bradbury singled out George Arliss as the model for
us all to follow. She approved as well of Mary Astor
and Ruth Chatterton. She claimed that Mary Astor
had studied with her, but the time and place of such
study was not at all clear—she was just one more
beautiful example of the triumph of the Bradbury
method.

Mrs. Bradbury shared her apartment and later her
theater-studio, which was lined with Japanese paint-
ings her husband had brought back from a tour of
duty in Vladivostok, with her sister-in-law, Miss Effie
Bradbury. A shy maiden lady, Miss Effie was exactly
the opposite of Mrs. Bradbury. She scarcely opened
her mouth and when she did her voice was faint. She
was graceful and smiling always and took part in all
studio activities. Miss Effie was a somewhat muted
reader, but when she delivered the lines of Blake—

> My mother bore me in the southern wild,
> And I am black, but O! my soul is white.
> White as an angel is the English child:
> But I am black as if bereav'd of light—

I sat open-mouthed; I thought that she was bringing us a message from another world.

Mrs. Bradbury, an excellent cook, often invited me to dinner before class. She taught my mother how to make pecan sandwiches, which seemed to me the greatest of delicacies. One thing that Mrs. B. could not, or would not, do was drive; that was Miss Effie's job. She sat behind the wheel of their giant Nash, her frail body propped up by several layers of pillows, while Mrs. B. from the back seat gave her incessant directions, frequently shouting at her as if she were a backward child. Miss Effie never answered, but hunched over the steering wheel and peering up over the windshield which she barely reached, she continued to propel the huge Nash on its way. I often went with the two of them out into the country. Since they both seemed to be magical creatures, I was not at all astonished that they started their picnic fire by employing what I had never seen before—canned heat.

To pay for my lessons, my mother made the costumes for the Nautilus Players, as well as the curtain for the stage of Mrs. Bradbury's studio. Mrs. Bradbury knew that we had little money. She also knew that my father had a drinking problem (in an unguarded moment my mother may have intimated that this was the reason for his lowly position in the Army) and she certainly disapproved of drinking ("Doctor" —as she always called her late husband—had not indulged). But she knew nothing of our bootlegging operation. And although she disapproved of drink, she was not a temperance leader; she had other fish to fry. But overnight temperance became her most important concern.

The reason was that the Woman's Christian Temperance Union (W.C.T.U.) of St. Louis was planning to offer a medal for oratory, and she was determined that her star pupil would win it. I was soon locked up again with the vapors of my bedroom (I could never use the upstairs front room to rehearse because my voice would carry down to the drinkers below), this time memorizing a dramatic—and wretched—piece on the evils of drink. The scene it described was one that I had lived through more than once myself, but the language in which it was presented was so totally uninspired that I could see that it would take a miracle to put it across.

The Missouri W.C.T.U. had recently placed in the schools of the state 20,000 copies of "A Syllabus in Alcohol Education." It distributed also booklets of selections to be memorized for the oratory contest. There were pieces called "The Guilty Man"; "The Rescue"; "My Car—and Whiskey—Killed a Baby," as told to Kenneth Crist by a San Quentin Convict; "Quicksand"; and "Shall Appetite Rule?" Another was entitled "Who Stole Cassio's Brain? (Based on Scene III, Act II of 'Othello')" by E. Wayne Stahl:

> Come now, friend Cassio, never think
> There's any harm in just one drink,—
> Just one: this is a night of glee,
> Which we must mark with revelry.
> Oh, do not be of mournful carriage;
> We celebrate the happy marriage
> Of noble Desdemona fair
> To great Othello, and declare

Also our joy that wars are done,
Because the Turkish fleet is gone.
So won't you take a drink,—just one?...

The selection that Mrs. Bradbury had chosen for me
was "The Tragedy of Payday" by Grace O. Cromer.

The contest was held in the auditorium of one of
the high schools. Vera Atkinson, who had acted with
me in a number of plays at Mrs. Bradbury's studio,
had been persuaded to enter the W.C.T.U. contest as
well with a selection that opened: "Human selfishness
defeats its own ends and ultimately loses all it strives
to obtain." My piece began: "It was Saturday evening
payday—a day that for the last few months had been
one of great anxiety, and sometimes worse, in that
little house. Would Daddy get home safely, and with
his wages? Quite often lately he didn't get any farther
than the corner saloon, where he remained till all his
money was gone, then late in the night he would come
staggering in to be undressed and put to bed." It was
clear to me that I would have to pull out all the stops,
summon up all my hours of training, and call on every
passionate fiber in my body to put across such uninspired prose.

In its *Approved Selections* the W.C.T.U. advised
the judges of the oratory contest that "absolutely
nothing but ability in rendering the declamation or
vocal selection is to be considered." They were to
mark on the scale of ten and use fractions where desir-
able. Contestants were to be judged on articulation,
gesture, memory, the ability to recite without hesitation, and general effect. General effect, the judges
were advised, "includes all that makes an address
telling—an intelligent conception of the selection,
sympathy with the sentiment, inflection, attitude, sus-

tained force, facial expression—and shall not be measured by applause." Apparently I satisfied them on all counts, and carried the day. Little did the ladies of the W.C.T.U. realize when they presented me with their silver medal for oratory that the suit I wore to the contest had been paid for by my father's home brew and bootleg whiskey.

It was not long before I looked down the street and saw our neighbor, Sergeant Grimble, making his way up the hill from Singer's, with legal 3.2 percent beer sloshing in a tin bucket. The Noble Experiment had failed, and our bootlegging days would soon be over.

PART TWO

To those within a system, the outside reality tends to pale and disappear.

—John Gall, *Systemantics: How Systems Work and Especially How They Fail*

You are one of our fathers. You have fought by the side of the great Washington. We will receive here your hand as that of a friend and father. We have always walked in the pure feelings of peace, and it is this feeling which has caused us to visit you here. We present you pure hands—hands that have never been stained with the blood of Americans. We live in a country far from this, where the sun darts his perpendicular rays upon us. We have had the French, the Spaniards and the English for neighbors; but now we have only the Americans; in the midst and with whom we live as friends and brothers.

—Chief Moshulatubbee, Head of the Choctaw Nation, to General Lafayette, Washington, 1824

9

DUGDEMONA AND DUMAS:
WHERE WE CAME FROM

Dugdemona and Dumas—the names resound through the long complex corridors of my childhood, sometimes with a faint and pretty tinkle, then with a deep mysterious and religious fervor, and finally with a dark and dominant funereal sound. It was many years before I saw the words and when I did they had none of the charm that they held for my youthful ear: the sound came first. *Dug-de-moan-ee* with the stress, of course, on *moan*. *Dugdemoanee* it was—and the last syllables if said quickly were transformed into: *money —money—money. Dugdemoney. Dugdemoney Swamp!* And I saw it always in my mind's eye as a bayou where the fierce sunlight filtered through the bearded trees and leapt back in bright coins from the black mirror of the water. Actually Dugdemona is a river that flows from the northwest diagonally through Winn Parish in north central Louisiana, where I was born and my father before me, to the southeast corner. The name became associated for me with the River des Pères in South St. Louis, pronounced "River Dee Pair," and the River Des Moines, pronounced by everyone "River Dee Money." When I began to learn French and got to know something of the background of Louisiana, I associated the small rivers of my boyhood —emptying into the ever-dominant Mississippi—with the exploring French priests, their habits as black as their waters. Dugdemona I began to think of—or did someone tell me?—as a corruption of "Duc des Moines," but that is probably a false etymology. Dugdemona appears to be an Indian name whose meaning has been lost.

And *Dumas*—pronounced *Doom - us*, a spondee—a small town in southern Arkansas, southeast of Pine Bluff and due east of Star City, where my mother was born, in Desha County, about twenty miles from where the Arkansas River flows into the Mississippi. I was never there, but the scene that took place long ago is as clear to me as if it had happened yesterday. My maternal grandfather George Washington Campster ran a little store in Walnut Lake, near Dumas. He went off from time to time to Oklahoma to buy up cattle and drive them back to Arkansas, where he had a slaughterhouse at Pine Bluff. Once when he returned with a herd of cattle, a steer took out after him: his children watched from the porch of his store in Dumas, while men rushed out and roped the steer. On this occasion he was saved. But at a later time he did not have the same luck. He had gone off again to Oklahoma and returned again with a herd of cattle. He took his son Floyd with him, and his older daughters, Effie and Catherine, tended the store while he was away. It was a hot midsummer day, so hot that the dust from the hooves of the cattle rose up to mingle with the cottony haze of light to form a kind of cocoon of heat around the cattlemen. Swathed as if in white bandages of heat, Grandfather fell by the wayside. They carried him, a tall, ruddy six-footer, with blue eyes and a reddish bristling moustache, into the cool of a saloon in Dumas. They laid him on the floor and, loosening the white bandages of heat in the cool interior, poured ice water down his throat. He was dead within ten days at the age of fifty-three. My mother, eight years old when he died, remembered for a long time the presents he brought her and the bristles of his moustache when he kissed her. He left two sons, the elder Floyd, who had accompanied him on his final trip, and his namesake, born two months after his death, as well as six daughters. Two other sons had died in infancy.

Dugdemona and Dumas—their sounds gave me a sense of the South from which I had come. Traveling south by train was like traveling into a dream. The train left Union Station in St. Louis in the evening, and the next morning I awoke to a wholly new and different world. The brown, rolling hills of the Ozarks gave way to the broad flat cottonfields of the Mississippi Delta. It seemed at once that there was an opening up and out, more air to breathe, more sun, more space. A mailbox leaning in an open field was a silver hand reaching up from the dark interior of the earth. Arkansas—Pine Bluff and its environs—was all light and flowers, but Louisiana was a complete dream landscape. The Spanish moss hanging from the cypresses and the cypress knees protruding from the dark water were like the limestone formations of the Missouri caverns brought into light and air. No Gothic cathedral could ever offer more intricate and heavenly vistas; no rose window was more splendid than the sunlight filtering through the bearded oaks. The rolling hills of Winn Parish possessed one of the finest long-leaf pine forests in the country. The great trees, towering fifty, seventy, eighty feet above the ground, impressed W.T. Norman on his arrival in 1896: "Long straw pines, as thick as they could stand, as far as the eye could see, the waxy green needles, glistening in the sun, the fallen brown straw forming a carpet through the forest and over the little roads winding through them." I went over those roads as a ten-year-old with my uncle Eric in his Model-T to Dodson and Gaar's Mill, where my grandparents had first settled. On the edge of such a forest I helped my Uncle George clear the land on my grandfather's farm in Winnfield, where I was born, and where the smell of hot biscuits and gravy, black-eyed peas, and fried okra greeted us when we came back to my grand-mother's table in the evening.

Winn Parish, the seat of which is Winnfield, lies almost at the geographic center of the state. Natchi-toches, some forty miles southwest of Winnfield, is the oldest town in Louisiana. St. Denis, who founded the French colony at Natchitoches in 1710, blazed the road from St. Maurice on the Red River across southern Winn Parish on east to Fort Rosalie (Natchez); this road became the famous Camino Real leading into Texas. Although not far from the oldest town in the state, Winn Parish itself was settled rela-tively late, and the families of my grandmother and grandfather were among the first settlers. The parish of Winn was created in 1852 out of portions of the parishes of Catahoula, Natchitoches, and Rapides. The name first proposed was Dugdemona, which would certainly have been more appropriate, but in the end it took its name from one of the families of the parish and from the lawyer who drew up the act creating it. In the early 1850's Michael Gaar led a migration of settlers from the Georgia counties around Atlanta. He established a trading post, a gristmill, a cotton gin, and a sawmill at Gaar's Mill, north of Winnfield. The Gaars were friends of my great-grand-father James Faith, and they urged him to leave Georgia and come on to Louisiana.

In 1857 James Faith and his family, along with eleven other families, left Henry County, Georgia, in ox-drawn and horse-drawn wagons, and were seven weeks on the road. They stopped first with Toby Gaar in Plankville, near Ruston, and then moved south to Gaar's Mill. James Faith, a blacksmith and mechanic, set up shop. Although he liked the country, he did not want his children to grow up in ignorance. Since there was no church and no school nearer than Sikes, he was planning to move back to Georgia, but he lived only two years after his arrival at Gaar's Mill and his widow elected to remain. The wife of James Faith was a Willkie, born in Scotland, who had landed at Charleston, South Carolina. The family of James Faith may have also landed at Charleston, perhaps also from Scotland, but I am not sure. They may have been French Huguenots, who anglicized the original spelling of their name, La Foi.

What persuaded these people to stop in Winn Parish and not to go on to Texas, as some of them had originally planned to do? Certainly the abundance of game and the fine country had something to do with it. The story was often told in my family that the settlers had stopped because their animals needed salt, and there was an ample supply of it in Winn Parish. Indeed, the early French explorers found the Indians thereabouts transporting salt in their pirogues. Legend has it that when De Soto was dying north of Winn Parish near present-day Jonesboro, he sent scouts to the Indians south of him to bring the salt that he thought might save his life. There are several salt domes in the parish, and the Carey Salt Company for years operated a salt mine there. It ceased operations some time ago when it was flooded.

At the time of the first settlement, exploitation of the mineral resources was far from the minds of the settlers: they were farmers and afterward lumbermen. Later, however, a marble quarry was opened on the edge of Winnfield, and through the years there has been constant exploration for oil, which has recently intensified. Between Winnfield and Tullos a number of wells, twelve or thirteen hundred feet deep, pump ten to fifteen barrels a day. In 1977 in the area of Calvin, north and west of Winnfield, a well at roughly fourteen thousand feet came in producing some three hundred barrels a day, and the oil companies have moved in quickly to lease the land. One driller has called this one of the greatest oil strikes he has ever encountered.

Colonel Samuel Henry Lockett, in his topographical survey of Louisiana, which he began in 1869, describes Winn Parish as one of the "piny woods parishes, quite open with but little underbrush. The surface is covered with a coarse grass that makes a pretty fair pasturage in the spring. Throughout the whole region there are numerous clear, bold streams of pure water, all of them abounding in fish, and many of them affording fine mill sites, and water power sufficient for factory purposes.... The inhabitants of the Piny Woods are proverbially poor, honest, moral, virtuous, simple-hearted, and hospitable. In some neighborhoods that I passed through I found little communities banded together by kinship or long friendship with many of the evidences of thrift, comfort, and prosperity around them."

The family of my grandfather William Austin Smith also came originally from Georgia and the Carolinas, but it took a longer time to reach the piny woods of northern Louisiana. My great-great-grandfather Samuel Smith came to Choudrant, Louisiana, in Jackson Parish before the Civil War. One of his sons had married and remained in Mississippi. Another son, my great-grandfather James Freeman Smith, had married Mary Wilson of the Mississippi Delta against the wishes of her father, a wealthy landowner, and she moved with him to Choudrant. He died there at the age of fifty-two. On his death, Mary's father offered to have her return to Mississippi, but she refused. She remained in Choudrant and married again, this time a Pruett. (Mary Wilson was of the family of Woodrow Wilson, who wrote to my Mississippi cousins from the White House verifying this connection.) Mary Wilson's second husband was, according to family accounts, a tyrannical slave-owner who beat his slaves. In any event, my grandfather was made very unhappy by him, and when the war came, he ran off at the age of fourteen and joined the Confederate Army. He played the fife, carried water, and tended the horses of his cavalry regiment. The roll of Louisiana Confederate soldiers shows a William Smith, a private in F Company of the Second Louisiana Cavalry. If this is he, he was captured at Natchitoches in March 1864, taken to New Orleans, and exchanged at Red River Landing in July 1864. I now own the fife that he played, an instrument worn smooth by long handling.

My father, with a penchant for intrigue, always persisted in believing that his father had been a spy and had actually served in the Union Army. There was certainly much anti-secessionist sentiment in northern Louisiana. In New Orleans at the beginning of the war representatives of Winn Parish voted against seceding from the Union and refused to go along to make the vote unanimous. The Parish is thus on record as never having left the Union. Once Louisiana joined the Confederacy, Winn Parish furnished a good number of men to the Confederate Army. I was brought up with a constant awareness that my family on both sides had been among the defeated. Yet at Jefferson Barracks my father had me memorize Lincoln's Gettysburg address when I was a small boy. Although I loved its rolling rhetoric, I scarcely understood a word of it. My father must have thought of it as a kind of valedictory statement that somehow might help to heal the open wound of the terrible conflict, the memory of which we lived with every day.

Whatever he had done during the war, my grandfather never spoke of it afterward. He was back in Winnfield as postmaster of the town at the age of twenty-one. He held the position during the years 1868 and 1869, at which time he also operated a saloon and general store. I have before me as I write the account book that he kept during these years. Each customer was given a page, and a careful tab was kept of all his purchases. The account book is a thin book with marbled paper on the covers, and the accounts are carefully kept in a beautiful hand. The main items offered were drinks (whiskey)—usually noted as "Dks"—and oysters. Few accounts are marked "Paid" or "Paid in Full." He seems not to have made very much money either as postmaster or saloon-keeper, but he was to go on to be one of the most respected men of the town. When Winnfield was incorporated, he was one of three general councilmen named to run it, and in 1888 he was named Justice of the Peace of the Eighth Ward (the district around Gaar's Mill, where he had first settled). He was also road commissioner. He ended up being fairly prosperous according to local standards, but his beginnings must have been modest indeed. Winnfield was a Fifth Class Post Office, a classification that was discontinued in 1874. The salary in a Fifth Class Office could not exceed $300 annually, but the Winnfield Post Office must have had difficulty even maintaining the position of Fifth Class. My grandfather's quarterly report for the period from July 1 to September 30, 1868, which my uncle George later forwarded to the Postmaster General in Washington, shows that he had sold stamps, envelopes, and wrappers (there was no parcel post) to the value of $32.65 and that his salary for the quarter was $9.50.

My grandfather died when I was three years old, but he stamped his image so indelibly on all those who knew him that I felt growing up that he was the one person in the family with whom I could readily identify. I treasured my mother's descriptions of him. As a young bride she had spent hours in his company, and since she had left school at the age of thirteen to go to work, she felt that her father-in-law had taught her everything she knew. He was self-educated, but he managed to teach himself a good deal, and I was fascinated by the leather-bound books of law and history that as a boy I found on the shelves of his house. One of the few photographs of him that I own shows him with a derby hat that is tilted back slightly on his head and a goatee neatly trimmed; there is a sparkle in his eye and a faint smile on his lips. He had a slight build, fair complexion, reddish hair, blue eyes, and considerable Irish charm.

He married the first time Lucy Gaar, and had one son by her. But the marriage did not work out, and they were divorced after only three years. Divorce in the strict Protestant society that then constituted Winn Parish was in itself a daring thing to undertake. His first wife must have been a strong-willed woman, indeed so strong-willed that their temperaments were sure to clash. My grandfather believed that she had made some damaging statements about him to a number of their neighbors, and he demanded that she make the rounds and retract these statements. They had met out on the lawn under a tall oak tree to settle their differences, and when he announced his demand, she turned to him and said, "I'll see you farther in hell than a buck can jump before I'll ever do such a thing." She mounted on her white horse, rode off, and that was the end of their marriage.

He saw his son by his first marriage constantly, but he never once, in the presence of his other children, referred to the boy's mother. If Grandfather had suspected that any of the children had had anything to do with his former wife, who became known to them as "Aunt Lucy," he would have been furious. His second wife Frances Faith bore him eight children, one girl, the oldest, and the others boys, of whom my father was the youngest. She was also a strong-willed woman who ran her household with an iron hand. My mother did not find her at all easy to get along with. I saw her last in 1938 at the age of eighty-three, when her mind was still sharp; she died four years later. In early photographs beside my grandfather she looks straight out and her jaw is firm and set in a determined, no-nonsense way. When my father was bitten by a rattlesnake as a boy, she took a knife, cut into the flesh, and sucked out the venom to save his life.

In 1900 my grandfather bought—from Hugh P. Long, the father of Huey—for the sum of $200, a twenty-acre farm on Center Street on the edge of

Winnfield. This property was the southeast corner of the Long farm of some 160 acres. Before that my grandparents had lived within a hundred yards of the farm belonging to John Long, the senator's grandfather. My grandmother did not like being out at Gaar's Mill and she persuaded my grandfather to move nearer to town. The link between my family and the Long family went even further back. John Long had come to Winnfield from Smith County, Mississippi, where he married Mary Wingate and built a home and a race track. Smith County was populated by settlers of Scotch-Irish and German descent who had migrated from Georgia and the Carolinas; it was named for Major David Smith of Anson County, North Carolina, a hero of the Revolutionary War. The Austins, for whom my grandfather was named, came to Smith County from South Carolina.

I was born in my grandfather's house at nine forty-five on the morning of April 22, 1918. My mother, who had been in labor for two and a half days, almost died. The attending physician, an old country doctor, himself the father of fourteen children, stayed with her during the entire time. My father was away helping build Camp Beauregard at Alexandria, and my grandmother and grandfather were busy with chores around the place. I weighed twelve pounds, and word of my birth traveled quickly. One of the first people outside my immediate family to see me alive was Huey Long. As someone later put it, if anything unusual happened, Huey was always first on the scene, and the birth of a twelve-pound baby to the wife of one of his old school friends qualified as an unusual event.

I saw Huey Long later only once, in Shreveport, shortly after he was elected Governor of Louisiana for the first time. He was then thirty-four years old, and I was twelve. We were visiting my cousins, Grady and Elsie Caldwell, and all the talk was of Huey. My cousins suggested that my father telephone the Governor and go to see him, but he refused. My cousin Elsie telephoned, and before long I was with my father in Huey's office, where we spent the entire afternoon. I had never seen anyone like Governor Long: in his white suit, with his dark auburn hair, his flushed face, and upturned nose, he was a powerful figure, right out of a book, bigger than life, and so he remained over the years, growing more and more into a folk hero as the stories about him unfolded in our family.

Huey grew out of the Populist tradition natural to Winn Parish. He always identified himself with the common man, and in doing so, he made his origins seem much more humble than they had been. Winn Parish had always had a somewhat unsavory reputation. My grandmother remembered that when she first moved there, her friend Toby Gaar in Ruston had advised her family against going down there "among the Winn Parish Hoosiers." Before and during the Civil War, the West Gang, a group of outlaws, had terrorized the region. They may have been the ones who set fire the first time to the courthouse. After the burning, Winnfield became a nest of crooked lawyers, all ready to reconstruct claims for the innocent victims of the burning. Huey Long boasted of his little "pea-patch" in Winnfield and said that the hillbillies there were no different from the hillbillies of Arkansas: "They all come from the same stock."

The inscription on the grave in front of the capitol that Huey Long built in Baton Rouge bears the inscription: "Here lies Louisiana's great son Huey Pierce Long, an unconquered friend of the poor who dreamed of the day when the wealth of the land would be spread among all the people." Dr. Harry Williams, the biographer of Huey Long, says of him: "He preached a rare and new politics in the South. He didn't talk about the past, the Civil War, Reconstruction, the 'niggers,' the 'Yankees.' He talked about current economic issues and he said these things mattered." It is difficult for those who did not live through the Great Depression to realize the impact of Huey Long's words and the effect of his radio addresses with their Share-the-Wealth message. Outside the North Gate of Jefferson Barracks the entire neighborhood would gather round the loud speaker when the "Kingfish" came on with his rich Southern rhetoric, which had its northern equivalent in that of Father Coughlin, the Roman Catholic priest in Detroit. When Long was shot, the common man felt that he had lost his best hope.

In our case, it was like the loss of a close member of our family. I was just beginning college when Huey was killed, and I was so naive politically that I understood almost nothing of what he stood for. For me personally, as my father's school chum, he represented all that my father might have been. I felt that if he had lived he would surely have become president of the United States, and then he would have been in a position to appoint my father to some office, perhaps an ambassadorship (Spain or Romania were the countries I had settled on in my mind). When the news came of Huey Long's death, I sat down and wrote a long letter to his son Russell, whom I had never met, explaining who I was and why I felt such sorrow on his father's death.

My father, overcome with grief, also put down his thoughts about the senator. Although there was any

105

amount of decent writing paper in the house, for some reason known only to him he chose a long piece of the brown wrapping paper in which the bread from the Commissary arrived and folded it down the middle. Then as if on parchment he wrote out in pencil these memories: "My recollection of the late senator begins at about age ten when in the classroom he could never keep quiet very long at a time. He would be snapping his finger for the privilege of sharpening his pencil which gave him access to talk to someone who owned a pocket knife and soon the teacher would become provoked and shout out to tell him to go to his desk and get his lesson. But when class time came and the teacher began asking questions maybe in history or geography he would have his hand in the air again and would prove that he knew his lesson almost perfectly. He was so good in fact that the rest of the class just stopped studying all together. About the time we entered high school there was a presidential and a state election. Huey would get on a box and speak in behalf of some of the weaker candidates as long as he could get anyone to listen. He liked to boost Eugene V. Debs, the Socialist candidate, who at that time got no votes in the South and not very many anywhere else. As our high school progressed a voice teacher, Miss Lee, was added to the faculty. She came to our classroom and wrote a scale on the blackboard and asked us to sing it. I sang so badly that Huey laughed out loud. Miss Lee, realizing that her first attempt at teaching a class was to be a joke, sent us both from the room. Strange as it seems, I turned out to be the musician, and Huey went on as you know. Before I finished high school I dropped out and joined the Navy, and after an absence of eight years I returned to the home town and found Huey newly married, recently admitted to the bar, and I can honestly say that he invited me to come to his office to study law. I declined the offer. A little later when I was married, Huey was a party to the wedding." My father concludes by recalling our meeting with Huey in Shreveport. At that time, when Huey asked him to name the most successful ruler of a people, my father answered, "Porfirio Diaz of Mexico." He explained his rather odd answer by saying, "My friends, if you will look up the life of this man and add a little of Abraham Lincoln and William Jennings Bryan, in my opinion you will have Huey P. Long." It is understandable why many old people in the piny woods of Winn Parish still share my father's enthusiastic picture and why they have a portrait of Huey Long hanging beside that of Jesus in their simple parlors.

Even though he was married, my father was drafted when I was just a month old. He went immediately into the band and was shipped from Camp Beauregard to Camp Pike, near Little Rock. When he was discharged, he decided to return to the farm. He raised peanuts, sugar cane, sweet potatoes, and corn, and was doing well. The only problem was that farming was such hard work. He soon decided that it would be a good idea to reenlist in the Army, and so in the fall of 1919 after he had harvested his crop, he went again to Camp Pike. My only recollection of the place was the terrible heat and the black tar paper covering the cantonment buildings where we lived that seemed to swell with the heat. When the camp broke up two years later my father chose to be sent to Jefferson Barracks.

When I was nine years old and a student at Blow School in Carondelet, one of my classmates invited me to spend the night at his house near Carondelet Park. The invitation was especially welcome because at the time I knew so little of life off the post. The house, a red brick bungalow with a brick porch across the front and stone steps that were kept carefully scrubbed, was not very different from most of the other houses in German-dominated South St. Louis. I grew in time to dislike intensely the scrubbed front porches and the mother-in-law's tongue in green china pots that so often was their only decoration. But then my friend's brick bungalow appeared to me the height of luxury. I soon returned my friend's invitation, inviting him and another classmate to spend the night with me at the Barracks. While our wooden make-shift quarters were cramped in comparison with their ample brick bungalows, I did have the woods right outside the door to offer and that made all the difference. After I had taken the boys over the secret paths through the woods I knew so well, my mother fixed a large meal for all of us, and everyone was tucked into the Army cots that she had borrowed for the occasion. I was in a room adjoining my companions, and they did not realize that the beaverboard partitions in our house were so thin that every sound could be heard in the next room. They began to talk about all the members of our class at school, their individual qualities, and finally about their looks. They decided first who was the best-looking girl, and then, to my utter amazement, since it had not occurred to me that I might look any different from anyone else, they decided that I was the best-looking boy. Their voices that reached me in the dark, as if through a dream, made me cherish them more than ever. I thought if what they said was true, then my good looks were a blessing heaven-sent for which I should always be grateful.

As the years passed I became more and more aware that I did indeed look different from the others around me, and by the time of adolescence, that appearance that had once seemed a blessing was clearly a curse. I realized then that I had only the faintest of eyebrows and that my eyelids folded up rather than back over my eyeballs as they did for everyone else. My eyes, I became convinced, gave me the Oriental look that prompted some of the toughs on the school playground to call me "Chink" or "China-boy." The normal pimply face of the adolescent is hard enough to cope with, but I found that I not only had pimples but also virtually no beard. Bits of fuzz grew only on my chin and my upper lip, with no sign that my beard would ever grow on the sides of my face. There was no one to turn to for help because I was not even sure what kind of help I needed: I became more and more withdrawn and found true friends only in books. It was in books also that I found what I felt was the answer to my problem. I read that American Indians of all tribes had very light beards and hairless bodies. What hair grew on their faces they extracted with clam shells. I thought of the only real Indians that I had seen—Big Ike and Little Ike, both of whom served with my father in the Barracks Band and came frequently to our house. They both had light beards, and although their complexions were darker than mine, still I looked more like them than like the other people around me. I decided that I *was* an Indian.

Throughout my boyhood I had identified with the Indians, not the Plains Indians of the films, who very early on seemed to me absolutely phony, but the Indians of the woods and of the settled villages who had greeted the early explorers; not the Indians of the wild war whoops and the tomahawks, but the Indians of the stealthy movement through the forest. I had discovered their arrowheads in the caves on the post, and I identified with them on my walks through the woods when I constructed my lean-tos of sassafras beside the muddy creeks, or when I moved on the balls of my feet over the underbrush, listening carefully for the slightest sound, the darting movement of a snake or the sudden thundering of a covey of quail:

Like brightness buried by one's sullen mood
The quail lie hidden in the threadbare wood.
A voice, a step, a swift sun-thrust of feather
And earth and air once more come properly together.

About this time my cousin Clara Louise came to live with us for a year. Her mother, my mother's eldest sister, Aunt Effie, had brought her five children up to East St. Louis after her husband had died from typhoid on an Arkansas farm. Aunt Effie worked in a woman's club in East St. Louis. She placed her two boys in a children's home, and her eldest daughter Erminie went to work for the telephone company. Clara Louise looked exactly like my Aunt Lucinda; although not quite so plump, she had the same high cheek bones, black eyes, and straight black hair. I became convinced that it was in them, as it was in me, that the traits of our Indian ancestors, whoever they may have been, showed themselves.

After brooding at length on the subject, I confronted my mother one day with the possibility that we were part Indian. She was shocked, not because she objected to that possibility but simply because it had never occurred to her. She explained once more that she knew very little about her family because her

110

parents had both died when she was very young and Aunt Effie and her older brother Floyd had never bothered to tell her anything. Aunt Effie might, of course, know something, she said finally.

And then she sat for a long time absolutely motionless, her black eyes fixed on some point in space. Her pose and her expressionless face clearly evoked for me the stance of an Indian woman.

The next time Aunt Effie came out on Sunday to visit Clara Louise, I put the question to her.

"Are we part Indian?"

"Don't be silly," my mother said. She seemed to want to make it clear to her sober and solemn older sister that she knew better than pay any attention to my wild notions.

Aunt Effie was a big, bespectacled, raw-boned, blue-eyed, humorless woman who already looked like the Gold Star Mother she was to become a few years later when her laughing red-headed son, a short while after his enlistment in the Marine Corps, died in the Philippines after the Japanese attack.

Aunt Effie was silent for a moment, gazing off into space.

"It's not so silly, Georgia," she said finally. "There *is* something to it."

My mother's mouth dropped open.

"What are you talking about?" she asked, all the resentment of her childhood rising to the surface. "Why didn't you ever tell me anything about it? What are you talking about?"

Aunt Effie was silent again for a moment.

"Grandma Campster was Indian," she said flatly. "But nobody ever mentioned it because they were afraid people would think that it was something else."

By "something else" I knew that she meant Negro.

I remembered being told by one of my cousins on a visit to Arkansas once as a small boy not to lick my lips or I would get "nigger lips."

Then slowly, as if leafing through a heavy family Bible, Aunt Effie reviewed what she knew of family history. My grandfather George Washington Campster, who died of heat prostration at Dumas at the age of fifty-three, was one of eleven children. His paternal grandmother Mary Townsend Campster was born in Ireland in 1800 and migrated with her family to Missouri and subsequently to Louisiana, where her son Samuel Raswell Campster was born. When her husband Henry Campster died, she married a second time, a certain Darling McGraw, whose antecedents were also Irish. I have been unable to discover whether or not the Campsters were Irish themselves. The first record of the family is in the French settlement of Cape Girardeau, Missouri. The name may originally have been French, perhaps Duchamp, the English equivalent of which would be Campster.

In 1850 my great-grandfather Samuel Raswell Campster married Catherine Williams, the daughter of Rebecca Tubbs Williams, a widow who had come to Drew County, Arkansas, from Noxubee County, Mississippi. It was through Grandmother Tubbs, Aunt Effie explained, that we claimed Indian—she thought Cherokee—descent. My mother remembered her grandmother Campster as a tall woman with straight black hair which she combed back into a knot. Something of a matriarchal figure with high cheekbones and a long face, she had an aristocratic appearance as she drove about in her own buggy. She lived to be eighty-seven, and my mother was always her favorite.

Aunt Effie went over all the Campsters and McGraws (cousin Benjamin McGraw had been a member of the Arkansas senate in the early part of the century). Most of them went back, as far as she knew, to the Carolinas and to Ireland. But it was my great-grandmother Catherine Williams Campster and her mother Rebecca Tubbs Williams who held my attention and who formed the real link with the past I wanted to know about.

I discovered many years later that Rebecca Tubbs Williams was not Cherokee but Choctaw, and of perhaps distinguished lineage. Her grandson William Carroll "Bud" Tabor, a member of the House of Representatives in the first Oklahoma legislature of 1903 and again in the third of 1911, put in a claim to the Dawes Commission stating that Rebecca Tubbs Williams was the daughter of Chief Moshulatubbee, the Head of the Choctaw nation at the time of the removal from Mississippi to Oklahoma. One of my cousins who tried to trace the Tubbs family found that nine Tubbs men had been killed in ten years in southern Arkansas and northern Louisiana, all of them doing something they should not have been doing. They were people who worked hard all week, got drunk on Saturday night, and went to church on Sunday. My cousin Lafayette E. Ikard also petitioned quite independently from Mississippi in 1903, claiming Choctaw blood by reason of descendance from Rebecca Tubbs Williams and Moshulatubbee, but because he could present no positive proof and neither he nor any of the other Ikards, Pettys, or Tubbses—so the court interviewer stated—showed any physical Indian traits, the petition was denied. The Office of Indian Affairs of the Department of the Interior, in replying on October 23, 1903 to William Carroll Tabor's claim, concluded: "The records of this office do not show that anyone by the name of Mashulatubba (*sic*) complied with the provisions of the 14th article of the treaty of 1830, and in view of the record the approval of the commission's decision adverse to these applicants is recommended." In other words, the Head of the Choctaw nation, who had himself signed the Treaty of Dancing Rabbit Creek in 1830 and from whom my family claimed descent, had never existed.

I was reminded of cousin "Bud" Tabor's claim in 1969 in Hong Kong when the Chinese girl operating the elevator of the hotel where my wife and I were staying asked us where we came from.

"Guess," I told her.

She answered without hesitation that my wife was American and that I was Chinese.

"No," I said, "I am American; my wife is French. I may look Chinese because I am part Choctaw."

And to myself, thinking of the Oriental eyes and the Indian traits that had turned up so often in my family (although they had eluded the Dawes Commission), I said: "One of my aunts looks exactly like Moshulatubbee, the Head of the Choctaw nation, and he may have been my great-great-great grandfather. But according to the Bureau of Indian Affairs, no such person ever existed."

At the time Aunt Effie's testimony was sufficient: while I was brought up on an Army garrison founded as an outpost in the Indian Wars, I knew that I had forebears on the outside and in the enemy's camp, and that knowledge gave me a new strength to face the limited—and limiting—aspects of military life.

10

THE STILL CENTER

Garrison life alternated between complete and utter quiet and total pandemonium; there seemed to be nothing in between. But even pandemonium had to end somewhere, and one sensed very soon that it would return to the quiet from which it had come: the pot that had been brought to a boil would be taken immediately off the flames. There was stillness at the heart of the reservation at the Old Rock Spring (Sylvan Springs), where clear water trickling out over the pebbles said over and over—as Elizabeth Madox Roberts has said that such water does to a child— "And do you think? And do you think? And do you think?" And beyond—at the center of the occupied section of the post—was the parade ground like a great manicured scroll on which would be printed only the music of the band or the sound of feet marching over the thick turf. In the barracks men spoke in whispers and tiptoed over the polished linoleum; far-off you could hear the clicking of heels at attention or the snapping of salutes. In summer the ceiling fans in the barracks turned slowly, wafting the tufts of still air back upon themselves, moving like giant brown bugs over the surface of water. Only the blare of the bugle at reveille, tattoo, and taps cut through the quiet: a stone dropped in a clear pool.

The other side of the coin was pandemonium. There were little knots of noise—the controlled hysterical laughter of the ladies at the officers' teas, the drunken male whoops against the slow jazz tempo of the orchestra at the hops at the Officers' Club. There were loud voices at times in the squad rooms or around the swimming pool and the clash and clatter of plates in the mess halls. But it was only in the gymnasium, on the playing field, or at the boxing matches that hell really broke loose. Atkinson Hall, which had been the main mess hall for the post, was turned into a gymnasium early in the thirties, and messes were established with the individual companies. The gym soon became a focal point of activity. Entering it during the fall or winter months when basketball was in full swing was a bit like being fired from a cannon, with the quick pounding of the ball down the long floor followed by the intense roar of the crowd. Men played company against company with all the energy of pent-up animals, and the others watched as if they themselves were making every play. Competition was equally keen on the baseball diamond, but the boxing matches were the most heated arena of all.

In the early twenties the Civilian Military Training Corps (C.M.T.C.) was organized, and every summer hundreds of young men came to Jefferson Barracks for a month to participate in military activity. They camped on the field across from the Western Front in rows of tents pitched on square wooden platforms. After the encampment only the cement buildings for

116

latrines and showers at the center of the field remained. When the tents and wooden platforms were removed at the end of the summer, kids from the Western Front would swoop down on the field and scour it for coins and other treasures that had fallen through the slats.

The sinkhole on the eastern edge of the field was fitted with wooden benches and a boxing ring at the bottom. Lights were hung from the oak trees. To the semi-circular grandstand on the edge of the parade ground was added another semi-circle of bleacher seats, and this became an even larger boxing arena. Fighting was, after all, what a soldier's life was all about. Men at Fort Bellefontaine had fought with bare fists; all during the nineteenth century officers settled their disputes by dueling at Bloody Island, just off the Illinois coast, across from St. Louis, while people lined up on both banks of the river to watch.

There was always violence just below the surface of military life, a violence that led many men to blow their tops, get busted and sent to the guardhouse. But it was only in boxing that physical combat was given official sanction. Competition among the companies was so intense that men were promoted solely on their ability in the ring and were prepared like leashed animals for the regular inter-company "smokers" during the year or for the summer bouts. The competition —especially during the terrible August heat which, even under the best of circumstances, put us all on edge—was so keen that it affected everyone on the garrison, including the wives who shared every detail of their husbands' lives, and, of course, their children. Officers' wives were not exempt; indeed, some seemed to find as much release in the boxing as the men themselves. Perhaps it gave a fillip to the dull routine of their lives—or did they find erotic stimulation in the contemplation of a male slugging match? Mrs. Ford, the wife of Major Ford, a supply officer who took over briefly as commanding officer of the post in 1929, was out every evening. With her slashed red hair in its mannish cut, a cigarette dangling from her mouth, she cursed like a trooper in a rich husky voice, urging her troops on. Her troops were not the men in the ring (although she found time to shout commands at them also) but her squad of young boys selling popcorn. The profits from the sale of popcorn went to the recreation fund for the benefit of the entire garrison, and Mrs. Ford was determined to raise as much money as possible.

So every evening before sundown I would appear next to the popcorn popper, where Mrs. Ford had pulled up her snappy yellow convertible. Along with several other boys all dressed in stiff duck trousers and tennis shoes, hair slicked back, I stood by the popper awaiting my basket of bags of corn and the orders from our commanding general. Mrs. Ford made us all feel that we were ourselves fighters about to go into the ring and whoever ended the evening selling the most bags would also win his golden gloves or his laurel crown. Actually our only reward was twenty-five or fifty cents a night and the husky approval of Mrs. Ford. But since she made us feel so much a part of the action, playing an important part under the white hot light, it all seemed worth it. More often than not, I would end up selling the most bags and go home late, exhausted and dripping wet, to drop my hot head on a cool pillow.

In the course of the evening I made my way through C.M.T.C. Camp with the bunks lined up in tent after tent and the men in all the disarray of undress

1. Jefferson Barracks in 1841, from *The Valley of the Mississippi*, by J.C. Wild (St. Louis, 1841). Photograph courtesy of Missouri Historical Society, St. Louis, Mo.

2. Friday afternoon review at Jefferson Barracks in the thirties; the Hospital in the background and the barracks, including the Band Barracks, to the left.

3. The Third U.S. Cavalry Band, stationed at Jefferson Barracks from 1894 to 1898. Photograph courtesy of Jefferson Barracks Museum.

4. The Sixth Infantry Band in the early thirties. My father is the second from the right in the second row.

5. Members of the Sixth Infantry at the rifle range at Arcadia, Missouri, in the thirties. Sgt. Boyd E. Layton, the mess sergeant of Service Company, is kneeling beside the baskets of grapes.

6. Regimental review, Sixth Infantry, at Jefferson Barracks following presentation of the Distinguished Service Cross to Capt. George O. Vonland (second from left), June 2, 1934. Colonel Krueger, commanding officer of Jefferson Barracks, (left), Maj. Tadeo Terriagaki, Japanese exchange officer (second from right), Captain Irwin (far right). Photograph courtesy of Jefferson Barracks Museum.

7. My father in Navy Band uniform, *circa* 1916.

8. My father during the brief time that he was a sergeant. On his lapel buttons he wears the coat of arms of the Sixth Infantry.

9. My mother at the age of sixteen.

10. My parents at Pine Bluff, Arkansas, just before their marriage in 1917.

11. WJS at Pine Bluff, Arkansas, *circa* 1925.

12. My brother Earl Richard "Richie" on Smith Avenue at the time of "Payday."

13. WJS with mother and Richie on Smith Avenue at the time of "Payday."

14. WJS on the right with Richie, behind the Boston house, the scene of "The Bootleg Business," in 1930.

15. WJS in front of father's tent at the Century of Progress Exposition, Chicago, 1933.

16. WJS with father at Schofield Barracks, Hawaii, 1942.

17. My grandfather William Austin Smith in 1868 when he was Postmaster of Winnfield, Louisiana.

18. Chief Moshulatubbee, Head of the Choctaw Nation, as painted by George Catlin, 1834. Photograph courtesy of The National Collection of Fine Arts, Smithsonian Institution (gift of Sarah Harrison).

19. This photograph, discovered in the trunk of my great-grandfather Samuel Raswell Campster, is of his eldest daughter Elizabeth Jane Campster, who is thought to have been the great-granddaughter of Moshulatubbee.

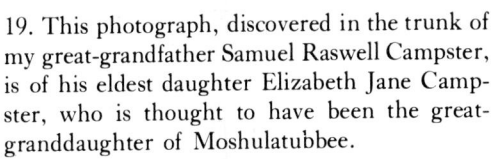

20. WJS, as a lieutenant, U.S.N.R., St. Louis, 1945.

21. WJS (left) with poet Stanley Kunitz (center), being greeted by Joseph Noneshvili, Georgian poet, at Batumi, USSR, September 4, 1979.

and all the attendant smells of massed masculine living. Under bug-studded lights I felt the whiplash of their earthy speech, most of which I was hearing for the first time. As in Michelangelo's cartoon, which F.T. Prince evokes in his poem "Soldiers Bathing," I was watching young warriors who had laid aside their armor:

> I remember how he showed
> Their muscular limbs that clamber from the
> water
> And heads that turn across the shoulder, eager
> for the slaughter,
> Forgetful of their bodies that are bare
> And hot to buckle on and use the weapons lying
> there.

But these were not soldiers breaking off from "some sortie of the enemy" but youths playing with the weapons that they would later learn to use in dead seriousness. Many of those frolicking there under the showers like boys at a swimming hole or stretched out on their bunks were destined to die in World War II. The field, where then they were preparing to attend a boxing match, would one day contain their graves, as the Jefferson Barracks Cemetery moved ever westward from the river to accommodate newly arrived veterans.

One place in the Barracks remote from riotous activity was the main Barber Shop, located in the basement under the old Post Theater and Chapel at one corner of the parade ground. Although the shop was below ground, it gave the impression of being just at the surface, with windows opening out into bays of limestone. Thinking of the place years later, I wrote:

The barber who arrives to cut my hair
Looks at his implements and then at me;
The world is a looking glass in which I see
A toadstool in the shape of a barber chair.

The years are asleep. A fly crawls on the edge
Of a broken cup, and a fan in the corner whines;
The barber's hands move over me like vines
In a dream as long as hair can ever grow.

I dreamed many dreams in that barber chair as I thought of the parade ground above me and of the life all around it. The order of the garrison and the disorder of life around me began to take on in my mind a new order. Every segment of the reservation—the whole of the Western Front, the company barracks, the officers' quarters, the fields and streams—all belonged to me at that moment. When I closed my eyes I saw each part, but it was not the place that someone else had given them but the place that I had assigned them myself. It was as if I had created them and they belonged to me, each and every one.

Next to the Barber Shop was the Post Library, an odd and uneven collection of mostly popular novels and detective stories. There, one afternoon, I discovered G.K. Chesterton's *The Man Who Was Thursday*, and I began to think of the world as itself a mystery, the work of a supreme commander, a man behind the mystery, "Who Was Thursday." I began to see myself also as a creator, part of a chain of creation that had begun long ago in some far place. I could see that there were always opposing forces at work in the world: where there was quiet there was noise, where there was calm there was violence, where there was peace there was war. And I would walk out

120

of the quiet Barber Shop and the Library, where in their deathly stillness I had felt spiritually restored as in the chapel above me, down the hall to the bowling alley: the thunder that greeted me would sweep all thought from my head. Then I would sit down in the chalk-filled air and watch the bowling pins shot down in the alleys like men machine-gunned in battle.

Another place of great quiet was the Post Hospital, situated on the far west of the parade ground and set back from the other buildings. The dark wide screen porches that surrounded it, hiding the red brick, and the shade trees before it made it seem a smudge or a great oblong shadow on the landscape. Jefferson Barracks had been an important hospital center during the Civil War. Dr. William Beaumont, one of the heroes of American medicine, had served as a surgeon's mate with the Sixth Infantry in the War of 1812. He had been stationed as Surgeon General at Jefferson Barracks between 1835 and 1840. In 1822, on Mackinac Island, while treating a nineteen-year-old Canadian trapper whose stomach had been torn open by an accidental gunshot at close range, Dr. Beaumont had revolutionized medical knowledge of the digestive process by closely examining the young man's stomach when his wound failed to heal. The results of his studies were presented in his classic book *Experiments and Observations on the Gastric Juice and the Physiology of Digestion*, published in 1833.

The corridors inside the Hospital were as dark as the porches; the brown linoleum floors were kept polished to a keen gloss. The wards were all white and gleaming, but in the somber hallways the ceiling fans turned like dark tongues, and the white-uniformed nurses making their rounds stood out like white teeth in the shadowy throat of a monster. I was to get to know those corridors intimately on two occasions, the first involving a friend and the second myself directly.

Much of the intense athletic activity of the garrison was emulated by the sons of officers and enlisted men, and I soon discovered that some of that activity was not for me. My father brought home two pairs of boxing gloves so worn that they were about to come apart at the seams, and my brother and I were set to sparring under the oak tree on the lawn. Although younger than I, my brother was of a far huskier build, and in any physical contest he was always the winner. I enjoyed softball, which we played regularly, but I was poor at baseball and usually found myself relegated to left field. More than any organized activity, I enjoyed swimming and hiking in the woods, right outside for us to explore, boys and girls together. We stole to the woods to swim at the swimming hole and to lie down under the sassafras lean-tos we built on its muddy bank. We also stole to the woods to smoke cigarettes that we stored away in caves, in tree trunks, and other secret places. When no cigarettes were available, we smoked pieces of grapevine or rolled cornsilk. But the greatest luxury was what our fathers called a "tailor-made" cigarette. Our fathers rarely had them themselves; they usually rolled their own with Bull Durham or Duke's Mixture. We would scour the woods for the remains of soldiers' pleasures: the "dead soldiers," as the empty whiskey bottles were called, were always empty, but a forgotten package of Camels or Lucky Strikes, even if it had already spent several days in the rain, was always usable. Hidden under a rock, it would be saved for a special occasion.

One hot July afternoon when I was ten, a frayed package of tailor-mades in hand, I stole off with two of my playmates, Evelyn and Nancy Langley, aged eight and nine. Their father Pvt. Jim Langley was a scarecrow of a man with more stripes on his arm than I had ever seen. "Pop" Langley had been an officer in World War I and had the stripe encircling his sleeve at the bottom to prove it. One day before long he would go to the staff sergeant who handled retirements and technically assume the rank that he had had during the war so that he could retire with an officer's benefits. I had become acquainted with the Langley girls on the auditorium stage of the K.C. Building, around which all our quarters had been built. I found them there on rainy afternoons hobbling about in their mother's old high-heeled shoes. Evelyn was a little dream of a girl with round dark eyes and smooth brown skin. I loved her, and the moments we spent together were the best that the summer had to offer. Nancy was blonde, an older, less pretty version of her sister.

With our package of tailor-mades, the three of us went into a cornfield on the edge of the woods to the south of the Western Front. On a warm day no place was more inviting than a cornfield, its cool rows unfolding like the pleats of a fan and leading to secret passages and rooms. The edges of the corn had already begun to turn brown in the heat, and I was aware, after some experience with campfires in the woods, that it was not the safest place to be lighting a match. When we had found an open area amid the corn, I cleared away a circle as if for a fire, and around it we sat like Indians for a council meeting. I explained to my companions that we should put out our matches and cigarettes in the cleared patch and not toss them near the cornstalks. And so we solemnly lit a tailor-made and passed it around, the smoke making us dizzy and sick with the first puff, but no one daring to admit it.

When the cigarette came again to Evelyn Langley,

123

she put it to her lips, let some of the ash fall on her dress, and the material, as light and flimsy as cornsilk, immediatley caught fire. She screamed, leapt to her feet and ran as fast as she could, the flame rising around her, and the cornfield flying behind her like a cape. We were right at her heels. When she emerged from the field, our next-door neighbor, Mrs. O'Hara, who had heard the scream, rushed forward, an Army blanket flying behind her, like a grotesque attendant at the birth of some corn goddess. She swept the screaming girl up in the blanket, a crowd gathered within minutes in the wail of the ambulance, and I was sobbing by the roadside. All I could see was the round black spot of earth that I had cleared: it whirled around me in the heat with a smell of tobacco and burning cornhusks and I felt that I was being drawn —with the flaming companion I loved—down into the center of the earth.

My parents took me into the house and comforted me as best they could. They put me to bed, and after a while, asked me to get up, put on my white ducks, and accompany them to the boxing matches. I went along in a complete daze: at the center of the brightly lit ring all I could see was a black spot whirling downward with my companion and me, and, with it, thin blue smoke rising from the cornfield.

Over the next few months while Evelyn was in the hospital undergoing skin grafts, I noticed a complete change in the attitude of everyone on the post toward me. While previously I had been popular and welcome wherever I went, I was now shunned and avoided. Nothing was said, or at least nothing was said to me: people just refused an invitation or looked the other way when I asked a question. I noticed the change the day after the accident when I took to Evelyn in the hospital a pair of small dolls for which my mother had made a change of bright silk dresses from the remnants on her sewing table. An attendant in the dark hall grabbed the box from my hand, looked glumly down at me, and did an immediate about-face when I asked how Evelyn was. Not being able to see her or to find out how she was made my grief all the more difficult to bear.

A joyous expedition with the Boy Scouts to the Gasconade River a few weeks later became a nightmare. One day I had been out swimming and fishing, enjoying a scene with all the transparent and youthful freshness of a Winslow Homer watercolor. The group I was with included Chuck Langley, the brother of Evelyn. During the day he seemed just as friendly toward me as he had ever been. But that night I turned down the blankets on my bunk and found an apple-pie bed, filled with cold beans and garbage. I knew that Chuck Langley had prepared it for me and that there was little that I could do about it, since the Chaplain, who was in charge of the camp, had been cold toward me from the start of the trip and could not be expected to listen sympathetically to my tale of woe. I knew that they all held me entirely responsible for what had happened to Evelyn Langley. I scooped up the apple-pie bed filling and sobbed quietly into my pillow.

It was at this time that Mrs. Bradbury appeared on the scene to enlist students for her expression classes at the Post Chapel. Before long she had me breaking out of my isolation and the barrier of silence that I felt around me and reciting pieces before audiences of admiring parents. One of the first pieces that I memorized was Frank Desprez' lively ballad "Lasca" with its tale of a "mad stampede" and its refrain, "In

Texas, down by the Rio Grande." The ballad begins:

> I want free life, and I want fresh air;
> And I sigh for the canter after the cattle,
> The crack of the whips like shots in battle,
> The medley of hoofs and horns and heads
> That wars and wrangles and scatters and spreads;
> The green beneath and the blue above,
> The dash and danger, and life and love—
> And Lasca!
> > Lasca used to ride
> On a mouse-gray mustang close by my side,
> With blue serape and bright-belled spur;
> I laughed with joy as I looked at her!

The joyous laughter soon subsides when Lasca, made jealous one Sunday by a girl in the Alamo, draws a little dagger from her garter and with the "sting of a wasp" wounds her lover. The stanza ends:

> But she sobbed, and sobbing, so quickly bound
> Her torn rebosa about the wound
> That I quickly forgave her. Scratches don't count
> > In Texas, down by the Rio Grande.

I had no idea what a "rebosa" (or "rebozo") was, but I could appreciate its being used to bandage a wound, and I loved the roll of the words. The ballad flies on to its dramatic climax: A Texas norther comes up suddenly, the herd stampedes, and the lovers ride for their lives. As the herd gains on them, the cowboy takes his six-shooter out of his belt and shoots down the mustang so that they may crouch behind his carcass to save themselves from the thundering herd. Lasca's lips are pressed to his, and her arms shield him

126

from the "sea of steers." He rises to find her dead, and the ballad concludes:

> I gouged out a grave a few feet deep,
> And there in the Earth's arms I laid her to sleep;
> And there she is lying, and no one knows;
> And the summer shines, and the winter snows;
> For many a day the flowers have spread
> A pall of petals over her head;
> And the little gray hawk hangs aloft in the air,
> And the sly coyote trots here and there,
> And the black snake glides and glitters and slides
> Into the rift of a cottonwood tree;
> And the buzzard sails on,
> And comes and is gone,
> Stately and still, like a ship at sea.
> And I wonder why I do not care
> For the things that are, like the things that were.
> Does half my heart lie buried there
> In Texas, down by the Rio Grande?

On the version that Mrs. Bradbury had typed out for me, the important words were heavily underlined to show where the emphasis should fall, and a multitude of little upturned marks after words indicated a rising inflection of the voice. So vivid did the scene of the ballad become to me as I read it over and over that Mrs. Bradbury's notations became literally the hooves of the cattle.

In reality, I was not saved from the cruel blows of the thundering herd that I sensed around me on the garrison, but the roll of the balladeer's words helped to soften them. Evelyn Langley recovered, and the following summer she was swimming with the others of us in the Post Swimming Pool. She herself was never unfriendly, but we were never again close companions, and I did not soon forget the accident or its consequences. One day toward the end of the year, while looking for something in one of my mother's dresser drawers, I discovered the pink front page of an October issue of the St. Louis *Star-Times*. There, staring out at me, was the familiar face of Evelyn Langley in her hospital bed surrounded by her dolls. The caption read: DOLLS CHEER FIRE VICTIM. The article that followed stated that Evelyn was about to leave the Jefferson Barracks Hospital "after lingering in the shadow of death for more than a month following burns suffered accidentally while at play." Her recovery was attributed to the fortitude of her mother who had submitted to two operations for skin that was grafted over the burns. But it was the remainder of that article that like a shot in battle simply took the top of my head off. In recounting the accident, the reporter got only one thing right, and that was my name. I was listed as the seven-year-old son of First Class Pvt. W.L. Smith. According to the *Star-Times*, I had been playing with the nine-year-old daughter of Pvt. and Mrs. James Langley "on the parade grounds when the boy found a match. He struck it behind Evelyn's back with the intention of scaring her. A spark ignited the flimsy material of her dress and immediately the child was enveloped in flames. Several soldiers nearby rushed to her aid and smothered the flames."

When I went to confront my mother with the article, I felt like a fencer, but in place of my helmet I was holding my head in my hand and it was speaking of its own accord, demanding to know why this outrageous piece had been hidden from me. She told me how, immediately after the accident, my father had gone to see Private Langley, expressed his sympathy, and had given him my account of what had happened, and in addition two hundred dollars from his poker table gains. When the article appeared in the *Star-Times*, both my parents thought it better that I not see it and that I try to forget the accident and concentrate on other things. My father went to see a lawyer, who advised him to give up any idea of suing the *Star-Times:* the most that could be hoped for was a retraction. But my father was too proud to go to the newspaper to ask for that, and a retraction would have made little difference anyway. The lie had been prominently printed and believed, and nothing could be done about it. I had learned something about the power of the written word.

I was to become acquainted with the Post Hospital from the inside on a later occasion. In the summer of my last year in high school I got a job as a dishwasher in the Hospital kitchen. I worked from seven in the morning until six at night, with an hour and a half off in the afternoon; the pay was seventy-five dollars a month. I stood most of the day over the huge sink, putting the dishes through the dishwasher and into trays where they were flushed off with scalding hot water. The worst moment of the day came when the attendants brought down the dishes from the V.D. wards. These were always covered with a green liquid disinfectant the color of absinthe; and I could picture myself, as I took the dishes out and sank them into the sink, as an aged and incurable syphilitic bending over a bottle of the stuff. We lived at this time at the North Gate of the Barracks. I walked about a mile each morning to the Hospital, back again to rest during the afternoon break, and back home in the evening. The final operation of the day, which I hated, was to carry out the long pan from the bottom of the stove filled to overflowing with hot coals and ashes. These were hard days, and I fell into bed each night like a boxer knocked down for the count.

In contrast to the absolute stillness of the Hospital corridors, the kitchen area where I worked held a reverberating crashing and banging that stopped only in mid-morning and mid-afternoon when the antiseptic smell of food, cooking in big pans and bubbling in kettles, would pervade the area and make me long for some sound.

One day during one of the brief morning lulls I was having a cup of the antiseptic coffee with the civilian boss of the kitchen help, a young man with the face of a peeled carrot, topped with hair like curled carrot peelings. Sergeant Davis from the front office of the Hospital came in to announce that all civilian employees would have to have blood tests immediately. One of the young C.M.T.C. men had fallen out in the ninety-degree heat. The sergeant didn't know exactly what had happened to him after he had been rushed to the hospital. He had had to be operated on, had suffered a great loss of blood, and was near death. Because of Army regulations—and here the sergeant's small black eyes flickered like the balls in a pinball machine as he unwound a bit of the red tape in which he delighted—Army personnel were not allowed to give blood to civilians, and one of the civilian employees would have to be found with matching blood. Off we all went to the lab, and then right after lunch I walked home through the woods for the afternoon break as I always did. When I arrived at the house, I lay down to rest and soon the ambulance siren was closing in upon my dream, drawing closer and closer until it was right outside my door. I awoke to find it really there, outside the window. My blood type matched that of the patient, and although other employees had blood types that also matched, I was chosen as the one most readily available and the one whose absence would least disrupt hospital routine.

The ambulance rushed me back to the Hospital, and within minutes I was wheeled into the operating room, where I waited in unearthly stillness until I heard the agonizing moans of the C.M.T.C. patient as he, in turn, was wheeled into the room beside me. His arm was stretched out beside mine, and when my vein was pierced and the blood pumped out and into his veins I had the sensation that the patient's groans were coming from deep within me. We were united now, this unknown young civilian in uniform, whose face I could not even see and who came probably, as many of the others did, from a farm in Missouri or southern Illinois, joined by blood, blood-brothers like the knights of the Middle Ages, united not for king or country but for the most ancient and honorable struggle of all, the struggle against death. I could hear the agony of his groaning deep within me as I was wheeled out under the slow-moving ceiling fans through the dark corridors, and I heard them still that night as I lay beside my real brother in our brass bed and prayed for him while the voices of the beer drinkers below drifted up the stairs.

I was not long in discovering the next morning when I arrived in the Hospital kitchen that the patient had died.

"How does it feel to be a killer?" asked carrot-face. "They shoulda known better than pump your filthy blood into the poor bastard." And he broke into a nasty laugh, the carrot peelings of his curls nodding.

The others in the kitchen joined in. "Killer!"

131

they shouted, and the sound of their laughter pursued me over the clatter of dishes and down the Hospital corridors.

It still pursued me that evening when I walked into our kitchen and found several beer drinkers gathered for their regular evening session.

"Weren't your fault that he didn't live," said a Bandsman I'd never seen before. "But they sure as hell owe you the money all the same."

"What money?" I asked.

"Everybody who gives blood is entitled to receive twenty-five dollars," said Corporal Upchurch in the same matter-of-fact way in which he took down orders daily at the Commissary.

"That's right, Georgia," said Mrs. Grimble to my mother, "and you shouldn't let that sneaky Sergeant Davis beat him out of it."

Feeling like a zombie straight from the graveyard —where, in my mind, I had been the night before with the young dead man—I stood the next morning at attention before Sergeant Davis and requested the twenty-five dollars that was due me.

Sergeant Davis's white face was a surgeon's mask; his black pin-ball eyes clicked into place, and his words came out like strips of carefully cut gauze. All I could hear was: "No requisition . . . no authority . . . I regret."

"You *regret!*" I was about to shout. "You're the one who put him in that uniform, you're the one who sent him out in the ninety-degree heat, you and your Army regulations—you are the *killer.*"

But I stood as if struck dumb.

"Thank you," I said finally, and walked back down the corridor to the kitchen.

11

SCENES OF THE THIRTIES

So encompassing was the military world in which I grew up that I scarcely knew that any other world existed. My brief visits to the South were reminders of a place from which I had come, but for me the present and the future were centered wholly around the Army. If I was to improve my condition, there was only one way and that was to go to West Point. For the sons of officers the Point was obligatory, and the son who failed to make it was permanently disgraced. For an enlisted man's son it was almost unheard of, but the possibility was held out to me like a silver lining that would encase my high school diploma and would insure my future. There were no secrets on the garrison, and every event of everyone's life was known by great and small. It was common knowledge that I was the head of my class throughout grade school and high school; I had even skipped several grades. After I began expression lessons with Mrs. Bradbury I often took part in church and Sunday school programs, reciting pieces on special occasions for Chaplain Zimmerman, who now took me under his wing to prepare me for the Point. If I kept up my academic work, he would see that I received a congressional appointment. I found school work easy and pleasant, and when I made an occasional mistake, it was never one to keep me awake at night. I loved geography, and when I gave a class report on Egypt, I pronounced Cairo with a long "a" rather than a long "i" sound. I did so because the only other Cairo I knew was the one across the river in Illinois and that one I had always heard pronounced "Cay-ro," like *Karo* syrup. But even if the work had been harder, I still would have done everything possible to excel: my parents had decided —and I concurred—that it was only through academic excellence that I would get to West Point. I did well in our local Boy Scout troop. And I didn't have flat feet like Jack Dalton, the son of a warrant officer, who had retired from the Army and built a house near the North Gate. I would look out every day and see Jack running through the woods to improve the arches on his feet. In the end, he made it to the Point.

Chaplain Zimmerman obtained the information booklet from West Point with its pages of sample examination questions, and I spent hours of my spare time poring over it. The format was familiar to me since it was printed in the small, standard typeface used for all orders on the post, for Army regulations, and commissary lists. The paper was so thick and tough that you could barely tear it, and it would burn only with difficulty: like the Point, which it described, it was indestructible.

There were brief intermittent sights of the world beyond the Barracks gates. I went downtown in St. Louis to see the floats of the annual Veiled Prophet Parade and to gaze on the King and Queen of Romania, when they also paraded through the streets, their procession led by the Sixth Infantry Band. Lindbergh in 1927 crossed the Atlantic in his plane *The Spirit of St. Louis*. On his return to the United States he visited the city and came to Jefferson Barracks. I was part of the crowd gathered at the corner of the K.C. Building and the Western Front to wave to him as he sped by in his black limousine on his way to the Veterans Hospital. The next day a tornado passed over Jefferson Barracks and cut a swathe two blocks wide and several miles long through North St. Louis. My mother had been to the Commissary and the Bakery that morning, and when she returned, the sky suddenly darkened as if the depths of the sinkholes had been swept up into it and held suspended, while the leaves on the trees stood out absolutely still, awaiting the great blow. We all waited in the midday darkness, feeling as if the breath had been sucked out of us. A few minutes later Mrs. Grimble came running from next door to report the tornado and its damage. We could breathe again, relieved that it had not come down on us. My father, with the entire Band and several other companies, was at the rifle range at Arcadia, Missouri, at the time, and they were immediately rushed back to St. Louis to do guard duty. The tornado had struck midweek, and the following Sunday we went up to see my Uncle George and Aunt Mary. The brick rooming house where they lived had been completely demolished, but they were unhurt. We walked with them through the rubble and I recalled the scene later:

> Glass glints; shoe creaks...A small child, I
>   walked after a tornado in the city, holding
>   my mother's hand.

135

The sky opened again above us like a wound drained
of blood, the pale edges folded in upon a pink
center;

I strolled beside her, and she seemed to spin off
from me in her dress of voile, her cartwheel hat;

And I gazed out on tilted and shattered telephone
poles, their wires trailing over sidewalks like
black spaghetti;

An acrid taste of burning bread hovered in the air;
the most intimate parts of buildings had been
ripped off, and here a bed dangled down

And there was the smell of buried flesh; and I was
sick and wanted to hide my face and run to some
green spot, gaze up at a proper sunlit dome....

It was a relief to return to the Barracks where all
was trim and orderly, where the lawns and buildings
were carefully tended, and where the violence that
lurked beneath the surface exploded only on payday or
in the prize-fight arena under the bright lights on
summer evenings. The routine of Jefferson Barracks
continued in 1928 with the C.M.T.C. summer encampment, its monotony relieved only by occasional
inspections and reviews by visiting generals. The popular songs of the twenties, which were wafted through
the windows of the Officers' Club at the regular hops,
seemed meant especially for this green place and these
still warm breathless summer evenings:

Ramona, I hear the mission bells above,
Ramona, they're ringing out our song of love...

Or:

> In a little Spanish town
> 'twas on a night like this.
> Stars were peek-a-booing down,
> 'twas on a night like this.

And the girls with bobbed hair, in bright chiffon dresses who strolled on the soldiers' arms under the oak trees above the river were surely the very ones spoken of in the songs:

> Ain't she sweet,
> See her coming down the street!
> Now I ask you very confidentially
> Ain't she sweet?

and:

> Yes, sir, that's my baby;
> No, sir, don't mean maybe;
> Yes, sir, that's my baby now.

Rose O'Neill, who had come from southern Missouri, about this time invented the Kewpie Doll, which became popular throughout the world, and the movie stars we watched at the post picture show had faces as innocent and sweet as those of the Kewpie. They wore the same rhinestones and dressed in the same fluffy feathers; and they all had names that melted into sweet nothingness in the mouth like cotton candy —Billie Dove, Blanche Sweet, Helen Twelvetrees, Dolores Del Rio, Janet Gaynor.

"The business of America is business," said President Calvin Coolidge, and the country seemed to be

getting on with its business far from us. In the summer
of 1929 I began to get a glimpse of that big world
where the green folding money that we saw at the
Barracks on paydays got scooped up as freely as if it
were leaves off the trees. Sergeant O'Hara received a
small inheritance from a childless uncle in Pennsylvania who had made a fortune in the coal mines, and
he proceeded to spend every cent of it as quickly as
possible. He purchased a long black Buick which
seemed as out of place on the Western Front as a
whale stranded on a beach. He took us all for rides
through the green countryside, past the golf course
and farms around the county, and to expensive restau-
rants whose decor was straight out of the pictures at
the picture show. And he began to buy up jewels and
objects that I had seen only in the Sears-Roebuck
catalog, which I studied by the hour on long winter
evenings. Mrs. O'Hara bought bolts of wine-colored
velvet and yards of lace, and enlisted my mother to
make the latest of frocks for her and her lovely blonde
daughters. The world became a round of horse shows
and prize fights and parades and picnics, a world
where guns were fired only in Chicago by gangsters or
bootleggers, at the rifle range in Arcadia, or at carni-
vals where the prizes were Kewpies or Happy
Hooligan dolls.

"Get out and get under the moon," the girls in
sequins sang on the tops of glossy black pianos; and we
rode the crest of a green wave under a pink sky, and
the women would be beautiful in big picture hats, and
we would all one day be as rich as the O'Haras and
ride in long sleek limousines and take endless excursions on the Mississippi riverboats. Our troubles would
melt in the froth of the muddy river kicked up by their
paddle wheels. F. Scott Fitzgerald, who came from

Minnesota, where the Mississippi begins, caught the
rhythm of the time:

> There'd be an orchestra
>   Bingo-Bango,
> Playing for us
>   To dance the tango,
> And people would clap
>   When we arose
> At her sweet face
>   And my new clothes.

When the bubble burst on Black Tuesday, October
29, 1929, the effect was scarcely felt by us at Jefferson
Barracks at the heart of the country, in the world
within the world, in the eye of the hurricane.

In the summer of 1929 Mrs. Ruth Price, a cousin
of Sergeant O'Hara's, came to St. Louis to visit. She
brought with her her two young sons, who were the
same ages as my brother and I. Ruth was a soft-
spoken, plain woman, who had inherited money from
the same uncle. She had about her an aura of melan-
choly (her marriage had broken up), which the quick
laughter and good spirits of her cousin, the sergeant,
did much to dispel. She also came to my mother with
yards of flowered chiffon to be made into frocks, and
she was soon taken by my mother's good looks and
Southern charm. My mother became her confidante,
and when she returned to her home in Allentown,
Pennsylvania, in the fall, she insisted that we come
east to spend Christmas with her, all expenses paid.
She sent round-trip tickets for my mother and father
and my brother and me, and we went by train to
Allentown to spend three weeks. Everything about the

train trip to the East was strange and exciting: the white tablecloths of the dining car, the folding beds in the compartments, the train winding its way through the long dark tunnels of the Appalachians and looping like a serpent around snow-capped mountains, higher and darker than any I had seen. The Price house was grander than any officer's: there were three floors and endless spaces in which to play. I became so involved with all the playthings that this affluent world provided—electric trains, erector sets, and Tinkertoys—that I was quite unaware of what was happening around me.

Sergeant O'Hara arrived alone, his usual jovial self, and assumed the role of master of the household. His presence there seemed perfectly natural. He was always around at the Barracks, and his wife had probably just not wanted to pack up to come with him. Sergeant O'Hara was still there with Ruth when we left Allentown after New Year's Day to return to St. Louis, and it was only when we arrived at Jefferson Barracks and Sergeant O'Hara still did not come back that I began to realize that all was not right. I soon discerned from my parents' anxious nightly whispering that Sergeant O'Hara was AWOL and that his wife was out of her mind with worry, not knowing what had happened to him. The situation was too much for my father, who finally divulged to Mrs. O'Hara where her husband was, and advised her to get in touch with Ruth's lawyer in Allentown. Sergeant O'Hara was soon back at the Barracks, where he was court-martialed, confined to his quarters for two weeks, and fined. I had heard all my life about soldiers "going over the hill," but I had always thought that the ones who did were the young irresponsible ones, not the old thirty-year men like Sergeant O'Hara. Because of his long and good record of service, he got off rather easily.

It was only later that I learned that he was infatuated as much by his cousin's money as by her. Since he had gone through his own very quickly, he was ready to help her spend hers. She fell in love with him, left Allentown, and came to rent a house in South St. Louis so that she could see him. My mother was her only friend. She died two years later of pneumonia with most of her money gone and her heart broken, not long before Sergeant O'Hara retired and took his family to Long Beach, California. My mother was at her bedside. She left my mother her clothes, some rugs, and some furniture. Her estranged husband came and took her sons, who were by then closer to my brother and me than our own cousins, back to Pennsylvania, and we never saw them again.

A few years later in 1933 I again ventured outside the confines of the Barracks when I went with my brother to join my father and the Sixth Infantry Band at the Century of Progress Exposition in Chicago. There I was more intimately involved with the military than I had ever been before. For several weeks my brother and I lived in my father's tent on the edge of Lake Michigan inside the fairgrounds, ate from mess kits with the Bandsmen, and slept on folding cots. I saw every inch of the Century of Progress, but nothing of Chicago. My mother came for about ten days and stayed for five dollars a week in a rooming house not far from the fairgrounds. She made herself a number of beautiful outfits, and we all had a joyous time at the fair. My father's unit had been chosen as the finest regiment of the United States Army to represent the infantry. Representing Great Britain was the famous Scots Highlander Regiment of the Black

Watch, and when the two regiments stood facing each other and the flags of both nations were brought forward, a spokesman commented that the last time the two had met was in battle in the War of 1812 at Lundy's Lane. They now faced each other in peace at the Century of Progress.

Being inside the fairgrounds was at first a great adventure, but I soon discovered that while the soldiers were admitted free to some of the exhibits, their guests had always to pay a fee of ten cents. I had little money, but fortunately the enlisted man's genius for beating the system came to the rescue. Sgt. William "Local Boy" Alden—with Lt. Alfred Bromet—in *The Story of the Sixth Infantry*, describes the situation: "Dimes were not very plentiful in those days, because the soldiers' pay had been cut to fifteen per cent less than base pay. If a private's base pay was $21 per month, it meant that he drew only $16.20. Out of that he had to pay $1.50 for his laundry and twenty-five cents toward the National Old Soldiers Home. That left him a net pay of $14.45 per month. That is not much money—but the Sixth Infantry showed the ingenuity which has made them the masters of difficult situations since our country's birth. A coin-operated turnstile was made to accept coins only the size of a dime, and it was found that the metal buttons from the fly of their fatigue trousers, when flattened with a hammer on a piece of heavy iron, produced a slug the same size and weight as a dime. Word got around, and the turnstiles reaped a sizeable harvest of fatigue pants' buttons plainly marked U.S. Army. At a meeting of the regimental non-coms with Major Urquhart, who was in charge of the recreation fund, Sgt. Henry Keating suggested that the major spend a portion of the fund to 'buy some new fatigue pants buttons, for the men

would certainly use them to recreational advantages.'"
I made use of many of the slugs that were collected
in our tent and became a familiar figure at the turnstiles.

My father received free tickets to a performance
of *Aida* at Soldiers Field, but my first experience
of the grand opera I had wanted so much to witness
was disappointing. I was placed so far back amid the
thousands of spectators that the voices of the singers
seemed to be coming from small holes in the brightly
lit ground, while a miniature menagerie of elephants
and camels circulated slowly around them. The car-
nival atmosphere of the fairgrounds soon began to
pall. John Gould Fletcher, the Arkansas poet, who
visited the Century of Progress that same summer,
saw the fair in his autobiography for what it was—"a
riot of overpublicized 'science' successfully mixed up
with a strong dash of sheer vulgarity, and served up
to the American public as the neatest and slickest way
of making money." I was unable at the time to see so
clearly behind the façade, but I felt uneasy being
locked up within the whole progressive business, part,
along with my father, of one of the prize exhibits. The
one exhibit that I wanted to see, because all the men
talked of nothing else, was Sally Rand and her celebrated fan dance, but I was excluded because of my
age. (Little did I know that Sally Rand was also an
Army brat from Missouri, a colonel's daughter who
had turned to show business to escape from the confines of Army life.) It was almost a relief that I returned in September to begin my junior year in high
school.

Horses and horse shows were still prominent at
Jefferson Barracks in the early thirties, and the local
papers reported regularly on the "riding breakfasts"

held for the officers at Sylvan Springs. But it soon became clear, under Colonel Krueger, that the Army was changing and that it would never again be the same. On April 22, 1932, the First Cavalry of the United States, the first of fifteen cavalry regiments to give up the horse, passed through St. Louis on a 750-mile march from Fort Knox, Kentucky, to Fort Riley, Kansas, for field maneuvers. The march was completed in six easy days of travel. Lt. Col. Adna R. Chaffee, pointing his riding crop at the crossed sabers on the olive drab sides of his tanks, was quoted as saying: "We carry on the Cavalry mission and tradition. We can't swim deep rivers or climb steep mountains, but with our speed and mobility we can find another passageway and carry on."

The First Cavalry and the Sixth Infantry came together two years later when they both passed in review at Camp Custer, near Battle Creek, Michigan, in important war games. Sergeant Alden describes what happened on that day: "The entire Sixth Army Corps reviewed one morning and were marched off the parade area to the south end of the huge reservation at the top of a high hill, . . . everyone but the Sixth Infantry, and their attached Tank Company, together with some elements of the First Mechanized Cavalry from Fort Knox, Kentucky. These outfits remained in the wooded valley below the hill. As the rest of the regiments and their distinguished foreign officer guests and the 'Top Brass' of the Army sat on top of the hill watching through binoculars at the activities below, they were startled at the sudden appearance of the Sixth Infantry and the other contingents emerging from the woods, storming the hill upon which they sat. It was a furious sight. Tanks, motorcycles with machine guns mounted on their sidecars, trucks with machine guns mounted on their cabs, and steel-helmeted, gas-masked infantrymen dismounting from them and running interference for them to positions behind huge boulders in ravines and gullies. Machine guns rattling, and rifles cracking, and the light cannons on the tanks booming, the whole show was over in less than ten minutes." Sergeant Alden, remembering that day vividly and carried away perhaps by his loyalty to the Sixth Infantry, reaches the sweeping conclusion that the regiment had completely revolutionized methods of attack in its ten-minute demonstration of mechanized warfare and that the foreign observers carried back from it the notion of the Blitzkrieg, which Nazi Germany would put so successfully into operation five years later.

Colonel Krueger, preparing the regiment for these war games, had intensified the activity at the Barracks. The society columns of the St. Louis *Post-Dispatch* on Sunday, April 29, 1934, carried an announcement of the schedule of summer parades: "A battalion parade every Monday and Tuesday afternoon at 4:30 p.m. and a full regimental parade, with the machine gun troops and supply wagons in the line, every Friday afternoon at the same time. The Sixth Infantry Band will give a concert each Wednesday afternoon and on Thursday mornings there will be special drills on the parade ground." While Colonel Krueger was intent on seeing that his regiment kept pace with change, he also revived some of the oldest Army customs. One Wednesday afternoon in April the Band played a concert on the lawn in front of the quarters of Lt. and Mrs. Daniel Hundley as a serenade to Mrs. Hundley, who was the youngest bride on the post. On a Wednesday in May the Band gave another concert in front of the Commanding Officer's quarters to honor Mrs.

Krueger, who celebrated her birthday that day. But for the marriage of his daughter Dorothy to Lt. Aubrey De Witt Smith on June 6, 1934, Colonel Krueger pulled out all the stops. The wedding was prepared with all the care of the most intricate military maneuver.

The engagement picture featured in the central position of the society section of the St. Louis *Post-Dispatch* showed Dorothy Jane Krueger in an almost military stance—staring straight ahead in what appears to be a long dark dress, her hands on her hips, a tight-fitting dark hat slanted to one side. Miss Krueger, the article stated, was an excellent horsewoman who played tennis and swam. Her engagement had been announced informally the previous week when she had displayed her engagement ring, a miniature of Lieutenant Smith's West Point ring. Beside her commanding presence the faces of the other prospective brides surrounding her looked pale and weak. Lieutenant Smith, the son of Mrs. Kathryn Smith of Booneville, Missouri, and a graduate of the United States Military Academy, was on duty as a student at the Infantry School at Fort Benning, Georgia; the pair was to be married in June at the time of Lieutenant Smith's graduation.

Monday and Tuesday of the week of the Smith-Krueger marriage had the highest temperatures ever recorded for so early in the season, and a few scattered showers in the area were not enough to make any appreciable difference to the men lined up in their stiff serge uniforms to honor the daughter of their commanding officer. The first military wedding at Jefferson Barracks in many years, it was announced, would take place with the proper pomp and ceremony "on the terraced slope overlooking the Mississippi

River, and more than one thousand guests, including all the officers and enlisted men of the Barracks and their wives, have been invited."

Up to the altar, covered in white and banked in ferns and flowers on a tiered platform, went the matron of honor, the sister-in-law of the bride, in pink mousseline de soie, with a pink hairbraid hat. She was followed by the bridesmaids in white organdie dresses similar to the bride's, trimmed at the back with rosebuds, and carrying bouquets of pink roses, blue delphinium, and baby's breath. Finally came the bride, in her heavy satin dress with a high neckline in front and buttoned to the waist in back with small satin buttons and carrying white gardenias, on the arm of her father in his highly polished leather riding boots and his Sam Browne belt.

After the ceremony the bride and groom walked back from the altar under an arch of crossed sabers held by the ushers and all the officers of the Sixth Infantry. After passing below the sparkling shark teeth of the drawn sabers, the couple mounted upon the spring seat of a Service Company covered wagon beside Pvt. "Pop" Higby, who because of his great white moustache was known as "Handlebar Hank." Pop Higby, who never wore the regular campaign hat but rather an old Spanish-American War hat, always drove the service wagon. He chewed tobacco, and it was his custom to spit in his hands as he took up his reins and urged the mules forward. For the wedding he wore white gloves, but those who watched him closely saw that he spat as usual into them before setting out. Around the parade ground time after time the wagon went to the cheers of the thousands of spectators, and each time it passed in front of the guardhouse the cannon was fired. "Sparkplug," Sgt. Harry

Becker's mongrel dog, darted out each time the cannon went off and lifted his leg against it, as he usually did at reveille and at retreat.

At a reception held afterward at the Officers' Club, the bride cut the heart-shaped wedding cake with the bridegroom's saber. While the officers enjoyed their wedding cake and champagne, the enlisted men and their families gathered around picnic tables the mess sergeants had set up on the edges of the parade ground. It was a day none of us would soon forget: the handsome smiling couple striding under the drawn sabers and then perched on top of the mule-drawn wagon represented the best that the Army could provide.

One of the drawn sabers under which Lieutenant and Mrs. Smith passed that afternoon was that of Maj. Tadeo Terriagaki, an infantry officer of the Imperial Japanese Army, who had arrived the previous January to spend six months attached to the Sixth Infantry. In his immaculate uniforms with their red epaulets and abundant decorations, he had become a familiar figure on the post. As I watched him at the Friday afternoon reviews or at the shows where he delighted in displaying his expert horsemanship, he seemed a bright toy soldier sent to add color to our olive drab surroundings. Major Terriagaki was made an honorary member of the Jefferson Barracks staff. He lived at the Officers' Club, and two lieutenants were assigned to look after him; he took part in all post activities. His fellow officers entertained Major Terriagaki regularly, and he returned their hospitality by arranging elaborate dinners at downtown hotels in St. Louis.

Major Terriagaki was at Harvard before coming to Jefferson Barracks, but most of his time there had been spent with other Japanese students. He still had some difficulty with English. Like many Japanese, he confused "yes" and "no." When charming, but puritanical, Mrs. Krueger asked him one day if he was married, he answered, "No ma'am, I have two children."

"You Americans talk mostly two subjects—A, girls and A Prime, liquor," said Major Terriagaki to his fellow officers. "You get your A and I get my A Prime and we meet at Chase Hotel." And at the party that followed, the Major always picked up the tab.

His fellow officers noted the major's penchant for photography; his subjects on his weekend photographic excursions were invariably railroad tracks and bridges.

Major Terriagaki also attracted the attention of St. Louis society. At the ball given by the Margaret E. McClure Chapter of the United Daughters of the Confederacy at the Jefferson Hotel in February, Major Terriagaki, together with Mrs. L. William Ray, the Invitation Committee Chairman of the Ball, led the grand march. While Major Terriagaki was in residence, Col. Shizuichi Tanaka, the military attaché at the Japanese Embassy in Washington, visited the post for several days in April. Major Terriagaki left in July soon after Col. Walter C. Short arrived to replace Colonel Krueger. When he was ready to leave, he went to the Post Exchange to purchase some dolls to take home to his family. When they were prepared for shipping, it was reported that they bore the label "Made in Japan."

Colonel Short, who entered the Army in 1902 as a second lieutenant, was given the nickname "Machine Gun" because he had written in 1922 a textbook *Employment of Machine Guns* and was considered an authority on the weapon. Because of his familiarity with the Philippines, Alaska, and Puerto Rico, he had been chief assistant at the Bureau of Insular Affairs of the War Department in Washington before coming to Jefferson Barracks. In World War I he served as a colonel on the General Staff and was awarded the Distinguished Service Medal.

It gave all the men at Jefferson Barracks a lift to think that the garrison at which they served was important enough to be assigned to one of Colonel Short's distinction. He was made a brigadier general a year after his arrival. A little more then seven years after assuming command at Jefferson Barracks, as a lieutenant general at Schofield Barracks, Hawaii, he was in command of the United States ground forces at the time the Japanese attacked. Although a congressional investigation subsequently showed that his superiors in Washington had withheld vital information, he bore the entire responsibility for the defeat and died in 1949, a broken man.

Where Major Terriagaki was in World War II when Lieutenant General Krueger advanced in the Pacific as head of the Sixth Army is not known.

Seven years after the end of World War II, on the night of October 3, 1952, Col. Aubrey DeWitt Smith, then chief of Plans and Operations for the United States Far East Headquarters, was found stabbed in bed in his Tokyo home. The Japanese maid, Sigeko Tani, testified later at an Army court-martial that she found Mrs. Dorothy Krueger Smith, who had been drinking, dressed only in panties and bra standing near her dressing table. The maid removed a hunting knife from her hands and heard her say, "I'm glad I did it." Lt. Col. Joseph Hardin who arrived on the scene soon afterward, quoted Mrs. Smith as saying, "It's too bad I didn't get him in the heart."

The shining sabers lifted above the handsome young pair on the banks of the Mississippi had come down on them both, and the pretty scenes of the thirties had vanished as surely as the white roses and baby's breath beside the heart-shaped cake on their wedding table.

12

BREAKING OUT

Early one Sunday morning a policeman found Sgt. Walter Payne of Jefferson Barracks sprawled in a gutter near the intersection of Broadway and Rutger, halfway to downtown St. Louis. His trousers were lowered and he was bleeding profusely. His penis had been cut off and stuffed into the pocket of his uniform. The policeman called an ambulance, got the sergeant to a hospital, and saved his life.

Sergeant Payne had apparently been discovered *in flagrante delicto* by an irate husband, who had taken immediate and explicit revenge.

The news soon made the rounds of the garrison.

"He was cut off at the front," someone said.

"They removed his bayonet," said another.

"They silenced his reveille," said a third.

On another occasion Sgt. "Tex" Schanley, one of the crack soldiers of the Sixth Infantry, went on board the steamer St. Paul after having led the Memorial Day parade. Midway on the trip, a drunken Schanley jumped overboard into the paddle wheel of the steamboat.

Word went around that he had contracted syphilis; others said that he had been rejected by his girlfriend; still others reported that "Tex" had taken his life because he was more blessed than most men—"built like a mule," they said—and too much for any woman. Several of his buddies accompanied his body back to Texas.

Sex and liquor were the two primary concerns of the enlisted man, and both could be had in places not far off the post, usually with less dramatic results. St. Louis in the twenties and thirties was one of the most notorious centers of prostitution in the country, if not the world. Brothels ringed the waterfront and downtown areas of the city, and immediately across the river in East St. Louis was "The Valley," covering several acres. Here hundreds of largely black women attended their customers in rickety wooden cribs. But the men from Jefferson Barracks seldom had to go so far; the prostitutes came to them. On payday they would appear at the streetcar station in their bright green and red satin dresses, wearing tennis shoes, and often carrying blankets under their arms. In 1927 the venereal disease rate at Jefferson Barracks was one of the highest in the Army.

When as teen-agers we made our way to the swimming hole, we would sometimes come on a couple making love in the underbrush. It did not take us long to learn the facts of life.

The wife of Colonel England, for whom my mother worked, presented her one day with what we always referred to as the "Arabian shawl." It was a colorful orange and red fringed blanket or rug probably originally from India, and for some time it covered the divanet in our living room at the K.C. Building. When it began to wear through, my mother gave it to my brother and me and our friends to play with on the lawn. It was used during one whole summer to make an elaborately constructed tent, under which the children of both sexes gathered on Army blankets during the hot afternoons to play cards and other games. Here the older girls of the neighborhood presided like the matriarchs of a primitive tribe. They took charge as if it were their prerogative, the guardians of secrets which it was their duty to pass on. It was here, under the Arabian shawl, that several of the older girls one afternoon told me and a girl my age (we were nine years old) to disrobe and display our sex to each other. On another afternoon I was shown how to penetrate my partner, and although too young to ejaculate, to enjoy that "funny feeling." Other secret encounters took place in the caves we dug on the edge of the road. The soft Missouri clay was easily scooped out and fashioned into any number of rooms. Over the structures we placed boards, which we then covered with earth, and in this way we had complete underground houses. We also climbed the oak trees and built equally elaborate tree houses.

My adolescence coincided with the advent of the automobile, which meant breaking out to explore the neighboring areas in pursuit of adventure. Sergeant and Mrs. Layton had moved to a house midway between the North Gate and the parade ground, and Sergeant Layton was among the first enlisted men to acquire a car. In his Model-A sedan he took us off over the countryside, and it seemed the height of pleasure to have all the familiar places—houses, trees, fields, horses—flying past us as we turned on those high wheels. Before long the cars began to multiply and young people who borrowed their parents' cars were off exploring what night life there was adjacent to the post.

154

Breaking Out

One night the Bandleader's sons borrowed the family car and took my brother and me to visit a brothel in downtown St. Louis. Too frightened to go off with any of the women, we stood with a number of other callow youths to watch a "Bottle Dance," in which a young black girl lay on the bed in front of us working a Coca-Cola bottle deeper and deeper into her vagina, emitting from time to time shrill cries of delight. As she finished her act, she singled me out, looked up, and said:

"Come on, Banjo Eyes, let's have some fun!"

I spun around and fled out to the street, feeling faint and sick. Other women, naked to the waist, were swilling beer from a can that they passed to one another as they called out invitations to men gathering around below the window.

Another evening we went over to "The Valley," where potholes were purposely deepened on the dirt roads to slow the passing cars. The prostitutes climbed on the running boards and entreated the occupants to pull up and visit them in their cribs. Our Model-A coupé wobbled its way through a sea of black breasts, while on each side of the road bare light bulbs revealed more and more pockets of dark heaving bosoms. The air was thick with smoke, replete with the smell of Bull Durham and stale beer, and from every side came obscene inviting voices and shrill mocking laughter.

Too terrified to stop, we slowly made our way back to the main thoroughfare, crossed the river, and proceeded down Broadway. Halfway to the Barracks the Model-A suddenly collapsed. The potholes had broken its axle. We had to leave the car in a garage and take the streetcar back to the Barracks. We had paid dearly for our descent into the Valley.

With the automobile, roadhouses sprang up near

155

the Barracks, and they also held their secrets. We went to one on Telegraph Road where the black singer offered up her song with a special flourish. While the piano player swept up and down the keyboard with his soft jazz melody accentuated by the thumping of the drummer, the singer made her way around the dance floor approaching each table to deliver a verse of her song. The drummer stroked his snare drum with tantalizing insistence as she swept up the folds of her long skirt, approached the table, and with her vagina picked up the quarters that customers had plumped down for the purpose.

"Some guys heated them up one night," said the Bandleader's older son, with a crazed look behind his thick glasses as he lit a cigarette.

We left.

After such exposures to night life, it was good to go home to a cool clean bed where I would dream of my beautiful girlfriend Geraldine. I had acted with her at Mrs. Bradbury's studio in several plays, and she seemed the most beautiful creature who had ever existed. The fact that her last name was Krumm did nothing to spoil my sweet vision of her. As I went to sleep I imagined that my white pillow was her cool cheek, and I enveloped it lovingly in my arms.

My brief but brutal encounters with women got all mixed up in my mind with my imaginary encounters, which were more protracted and more satisfactory, and the two became hopelessly confused. Like every adolescent I was living on an edge between dream and reality and sometimes I sank into what was pure nightmare. The picture show had been for some time, along with prize fights and basketball matches, our sole recreation on the garrison. Under the Arabian shawl we traded pictures of our movie stars—Blanche

Sweet, Dolores Del Rio, Bebe Daniels, Billie Dove—
and we learned where to send away for others. During
my high school years a new Post Theater had been
built beside the Hospital, and on summer evenings my
brother and I would put on our white duck trousers
and walk off through the woods to the picture show.
Usually we had canteen checks, which my father had
won or collected in exchange for drinks, to cover the
entrance fee, but there were times when we did not.
We discovered that the window to the toilet on the
side of the building was always left open, and since it
was at ground level we could just hoist our legs over
the window ledge and climb in. We would wait until
the picture began, and in the darkness find a seat with
our friends—a good proportion of the audience was
young people. It did not seem at all inappropriate to
us that our entrance to paradise should be through a
place of excrement.

It was in the woods that I composed my own day-
dreams and where, in a sense, I made my own films.
I would start off on a summer day with a bucket to
gather blackberries, which were plentiful, and in every
thicket I would meet my dream girls. In my imagina-
tion I lay with them on the wet edges of the creeks,
returning in the evening utterly exhausted but satisfied. I was beginning to read of nymphs, and I was
certain that they existed even on the edge of Missouri
sinkholes, although there they were more likely to
take the form of Indian maidens on moccasined feet,
half-clothed in what seemed to be Arabian shawls.

I was living on an edge dividing dream and reality,
and I was living also on an edge dividing military
and civilian life. This narrow division appeared to me
to be symbolized by the doors that divided my front
upstairs study room from the men in the Boston house,

who sat in the dining room drinking my father's boot-leg home brew and whiskey. The stairway came right into the front room upstairs where I studied, and the only bathroom in the house was immediately to the right as you climbed the stairs. To form a sort of shield so that the drinkers could go upstairs to the bathroom without entering the room, my father had put together a whole series of doors, one alongside the other, making a little hallway, with a real doorway at the end that opened into the room. The doors came only halfway up the wall and consequently did not keep out any noise. I hated the lot of them, and when I heard some drunken soldier struggling up the stairs, I half hoped that the doors would all fold quickly together and collapse on him. These doors began to represent the unstable partition dividing me from the vulgar aspects of military life.

On my side of the partition I had my books and my typewriter, which my mother had found some-where, probably at Klebs Pawnshop. At this shop at the end of the Broadway carline the men from the Barracks hocked their clothes on payday, and I made regular trips there with my mother to buy the suits I wore to school. The typewriter was an early model with the keys in the round. It did not work very well, but on it I managed to type out my first poems. It gave them another whole dimension; they seemed already in print as I read them over and over. One of them had actually been in print. My French teacher, Miss Edith Babbitt, who wrote verse, urged me to send some poems to a little magazine to which she had contributed, *Versecraft*, published in Atlanta. "Observatory" contrasted the vast serene heavens with the tight, restricted human world below and concluded:

Let them squeeze my soul with walls,
And tear my heart with iron bars;
But do not let them take the hole,
Oh God, through which I see the stars.

I was not quite so cut off as the poem indicates. We had recently acquired a radio, an ugly brown one, the color of molasses and shaped like a tea cozy. I would steal down occasionally away from my homework and hunch over it to listen to the comedy routines of Burns and Allen, while the noisy talk of the drinkers continued in the dining room.

I was now ambivalent in my feelings toward the Army. I was drawn constantly to Jefferson Barracks since it was the one world that I had always known, and to break away from it would not be easy; all my friends were there. When I acquired a bicycle, I would sometimes pedal up to the Carondelet Library near Blow School to take out books. I managed to get a library card for my mother, and I went into the adult section to fetch books for her, books that I always read myself. But more often, immediately on arrival from school, I would cycle off to the Barracks. My closest friends at this time were officers' sons. Dean Short, the son of General Short, was a classmate at Cleveland High School. Dean was a chubby fellow with pink cheeks and a lively laugh. In Sunday School, perhaps because of his Southern upbringing, he knew much more about the Bible than the others did, and was always quick and ready with the details of intricate Bible stories. He acted in a French play that I wrote for our class. The play concerned a beggar who turned out to be something else in the end. Behind the plot may have been my motivation to move up in life and to improve my social position. The Shorts certainly encouraged me, and I was included in the most natural way at parties given for Dean. Actually it was not natural at all, since enlisted men's children were never invited to the parties of officers' children. But Dean's mother, Isabel Short, a very pretty woman from Muskogee, Oklahoma, had a Southern grace and charm that made me feel immediately welcome. She arranged to deliver to my mother several of General Short's discarded suits. Still in good repair, they saw me halfway through college.

My other friend was Tommy Reagan, another classmate at Cleveland High School, the son of Major Reagan, the chief surgeon at the Post Hospital. Tommy had a wonderful quick wit, and we were together constantly at school, in the Scouts, in games on the parade ground, or at the Picture Show. To mock the way I rushed around at school from this activity to that, Tommy had nicknamed me "Bustler." I was usually the only one from the Barracks who stayed after school for any of the extra-curricular activities. I was president of the modern language club, a member of the debating team, and on the staff of the yearbook. Staying after school meant a walk of ten blocks or so to the Broadway streetcar line and then a trip of some forty minutes, changing at the end of the Broadway line to the Barracks bus, which had long since replaced the trolley. Tommy liked to kid me about my activities, but he really approved of them and was even at times rather envious of them. I persuaded him to stay after school with me one day for a debate. I put on a special display of debating skill for him. Our team won, and I felt like a hero as we rode back together on the streetcar. For the first time he expressed directly his complete approval. I frequently sat with Tommy in the officers' section of the Picture Show, the section to the right rear with white slipcovers on the backs of the seats.

We would stroll home in front of the officers' quarters after the show. The soft lights shone in the parlors, and the gleaming metal and silver trays flashed at us through the pink windows. His head beside me appeared outlined by the window lights like that of a young prince on a medallion. We breathed in the smell of new-mown grass on the parade ground, and our steps echoed on the cement walk. Tommy lived toward the end of Officers' Row, and I usually said good-night to him at his door and then turned to the right on to the unlighted road toward home. But sometimes I would persuade him to accompany me to the top of the first hill, along the iron picket fence that enclosed the grounds of what had once been the commanding officer's quarters.

General Kress had lived here in an imposing frame house on a bluff overlooking the river. The fence surrounding the house was made of rifles and bayonets from the Civil War. The gateway was flanked by two smooth-bore, muzzle-loading cannon standing on their breech with a cannonball on each muzzle. The cannon supported the driveway gate; two smaller cannon on either side supported the smaller gates, through which visitors would enter on foot. Between the cannon muzzles was an iron arch with filigreed ornament. At the crown of the arch was the emblem of the Ordnance Department, two crossed cannon supporting a bursting bomb. (General Kress had commanded the Arsenal at Jefferson Barracks and reported only to the Chief of Ordnance in Washington. His son recalls his father's remarking that the toast of the Ordnance Corps was "Brevets in War; Palaces in Peace.")

The Ordnance Palace, which no longer exists, was

mistakenly thought to have been the quarters of General Grant. Outlined in the moonlight, the Civil War fence formed an eerie, funereal backdrop as I said good-night to Tommy and plunged downhill into the woods, accompanied only by hoot owls on the road that wound up and down the final mile to the North Gate.

As time went by, more and more of my afternoons were taken up by school activities and my evenings by dramatics. Often I would go directly from Cleveland High School to Mrs. Bradbury's studio, first on Grand Avenue diagonally across from the playing field of the school and later farther south on Bates Street. On Bates Street for the first time she had what almost amounted to a real theater. She rented a small store-front next to a grocery store and had a stage built dividing the interior. Backstage she and Miss Effie had their one bedroom; in front of the stage she had all her furniture, her piano, and a folding blackboard and folding chairs. Here her classes were held, and when there was a recital or a play, the furniture was moved out of the way and fifty to seventy-five people could be seated. I felt that I had a personal investment in the Nautilus Studio, since my mother had made on her small sewing machine the green stage curtain.

My evenings were given more and more to rehearsals. We were putting on George Bernard Shaw's *Arms and the Man*. Mr. Wood, an unemployed actor, appeared one day at Mrs. Bradbury's doorway. His genteel, if somewhat shabby, manner won her heart; he stayed to dinner and she soon took him on as director of her dramatic productions, while she continued to concentrate on our voices. There were many late evenings, and long trips home—on the Bates Street bus and the Broadway streetcar. I would follow my reflection in the window of the car as it slowly clanged along, and I watched it detach itself from me and float over the familiar buildings and into the trees, merging with my mental image of the beautiful Geraldine, who was acting with me in *Arms and the Man*, the two faces drifting along in the mist, growing up like green plants opening out into an imaginary universe. I usually carried with me an anthology of poetry that Mrs. Bradbury had lent me, a volume that spoke of the new modern poetry, the kind of poetry that I was writing in my head. The lines of my poems were, I felt, locked inside me in a secret chest which I would return to the next evening and which days later I would empty out on a white page. Mrs. Bradbury had a complete set of the works of Mark Twain, and I borrowed one volume a week. The scenes of his childhood merged with those of mine: Huck stood beside me as I went over in my mind the building of a lean-to of sassafras beside a creek; he sat with me before the fire left by the hoboes in a limestone cavern above the railroad tracks; together we rode a raft below a wide sky down the great brown, terrifying, but ever-beautiful river, along which the streetcar was then inching its way, a clanging yellow bug.

I played the part of Major Petkoff in *Arms and the Man*, but the play's message of military blundering went right past me, or it may be that I had already received the message directly and graphically in my daily life. Judging by the stories told by the beer drinkers in our dining room, nothing in the military ever went the way it should and if it did, it was largely by accident. When I first heard the expression "red tape," I took it literally and saw in the squad rooms of all the barracks roll after roll of red tape wound around the feet of the first sergeant and the shave-tail lieutenant beside him. What was the meaning of the system if the built-in part of it was getting the better of the system, as it seemed to be from top to bottom? Was it true, as my father said, that it was only the sycophants, the "brown noses," who got ahead? Wasn't the order on the parade ground merely a cover-up for the disorder of the men leading them? Did I want to put on a uniform to regiment men and destroy the very individuality that regimentation was designed to protect?

On the question of the military our family was already divided. My brother was bored with high school and although he was bright, he took an interest only in drawing. The pictures he had done for a notebook on the *Odyssey* had won his teacher's praise, but most of the time he failed to do his homework. He decided he wanted to enlist in the Navy, and my father, who looked back nostalgically on his Navy service, encouraged the idea. What could be better than to have his son take off from school just as he had done and see something of the world? My mother was adamantly opposed, insisting that my brother earn his high school diploma before he did anything else. Only seventeen, he needed his parents' permission to enlist. When my mother was away one afternoon, my father signed the papers for him. It broke my mother's heart to have him go off, but he was soon on his way. His departure made me begin to wonder seriously whether or not I could really embark on a military career myself.

13

GRADUATION

At the end of my junior year I received the Harvard Book Award, presented at the time by the Harvard Club of St. Louis to the outstanding boy in the junior class of each high school. I had not even known of the existence of the award, and when I received it I started to think about going away to college. The book, handsomely bound in red leather, was the biography of William Clement Sabine, the acoustical engineer, by William Dana Orcutt, and it was for me a signal from the intellectual world to which I wished to belong. But my enthusiasm was somewhat diminished when I attempted to read the book. After several attempts I found myself unable to make my way through its impenetrable prose. My inability made me feel that I was letting down the Harvard Club, as well as Harvard itself. And I feared even more that my inability to appreciate this gift fully might mean that I would be unable to meet the standards of Harvard, if by some miracle I should ever get there. (I looked at the book again recently and realize that it was

Harvard that was letting me down: the prose is indeed impenetrable.) I made a special trip to the public library to examine a Harvard catalog. When I saw the astronomical tuition figures, I realized it would certainly take a miracle for me to go. When I looked at the tuition figures of a college closer to home—Oberlin in Ohio—they also seemed astronomical. College appeared out of the question.

About this time the Cleveland High School chorus, of which I was a member, was invited to participate in a competition with other choruses from the St. Louis area at the Field House at Washington University. We put in a long and tiring day, and we did not walk off with the top award. What was important was that I secretly felt, although I dared not speak of it to anyone at the time, that this was a turning point in my life. The Washington University campus was the very first campus I had seen anywhere in the world, and I could not have chosen a better one. Designed by the Kansas City landscaping firm responsible for the layout of the St. Louis World's Fair in 1903, it was and is an extraordinarily beautiful campus. Its granite Tudor towers, its brick walks, its front quadrangle, its chapel (modeled on the one at Cambridge), its broad green lawns and playing fields all were instantly a magical realm. It did not seem possible that such an array of buildings and such a powerful plant could be given over wholly to the pursuit of learning. The entire establishment, in its neat and orderly way, was not unlike Jefferson Barracks, but its buildings were ever so much more pleasing aesthetically. And it was exhilarating to think that here these green fields would be occupied not by squads of regimented men in uniform, but by students free to come and go as they liked. This surely was the home of the intellectual elite to which I wished to belong. When late in the afternoon the Cleveland High School chorus finally took its place to sing before the large audience. I was dizzy with excitement. I am not at all sure that my voice followed the notes exactly, but I felt that I sang gloriously as if by divine sanction. I had the odd, pleasing, and yet somehow terrifying sensation that while my voice was now only one among many, some day it would rise above the others and be heard in the vast realm represented by those stone towers and green lawns.

Washington University awarded a scholarship covering full tuition to the top-ranking student in each of the St. Louis high schools. I was aware of this opportunity because each year on the graduation program of Cleveland High School, in small print at the bottom, was an announcement of the winner. I decided that in 1935 my name would have to appear in that place. I had never thought about grades. I worked hard and took courses that interested me, and I usually ended up at the top of my class. In my senior year I wanted particularly to study Latin, but my adviser, Mr. Tucker, a teacher of sociology, was worried that I was already carrying too many subjects and was engaged in too many extra-curricular activities to take on anything else. Any increase in my academic load would, he thought, impair my health. I could not convince him that anything involving language I could accomplish joyously with my left hand (indeed, I proceeded to get hold of a Latin grammar and work at Latin on my own, on the streetcar on the way home from school.)

An assignment for Mr. Tucker's sociology class took me to the St. Louis slums. I stood alone for almost an hour in an abandoned building gazing out the window at the devastation around me—trash, garbage, broken bottles, cans. I found all this decay, this waste, these broken human habitations on the frayed edges of the urban world terrifying. The vision of that day has never left me, but at the time I was unable to react in any intelligent way to it. I could certainly not react to it in the conventional jargon of a sociological textbook. I made mental notes for a poem and then went back and wrote my sociology paper on something else that I could more easily deal with at the time.

Toward the end of my last semester at Cleveland High School the principal called me into his office. Two other seniors, both girls, were also there. The principal explained that on the basis of our academic averages the three of us led our class. Our averages were almost the same, separated one from the other by a few hundredths of a point (actually I was third). Since they were so close, the principal and the teachers advising him felt that they could not make a decision on which of us should receive the Washington University scholarship. He was sending our records to the university and asking it to decide. Word came back at once that it had decided in favor of the girl with the highest numerical average. I felt betrayed by absolutely everyone. I scarcely knew the winner, and she was undoubtedly intelligent (she was later elected to Phi Beta Kappa), but in her four high-school years she had taken courses like typing and home economics. The grades for these subjects should not, I thought, carry the same weight as those for the solid academic courses I had taken. Her record of extra-curricular activities was far inferior to mine. My contributions of stories and poems to the school paper and the yearbook, my prominence in the modern language club and the debating society should count for something.

The university officials were irresponsible in not having interviewed us all or in not having us take some sort of examination. And I felt betrayed as well by my adviser: an additional A in Latin, which I would certainly have received, would have put me over the top. And finally I felt that I had betrayed myself by not watching my academic average more closely since that alone was going to determine my future.

Since it was now clear that I would not be able to go to college, I did not want to rule out the possibility of West Point. That possibility seemed day by day less attractive, but if Chaplain Zimmerman could arrange for a congressional appointment for me, I would certainly have to accept it. After all, I had been brought up in the military, and one thing I had learned about that system was that, no matter how much you detested it, there were ways of beating it. I was not yet old enough or tough enough to accept this notion, but perhaps I would be one day. In the meantime, I had to make some plans for the immediate future. I enrolled for the summer course at Brown's Business School in St. Louis.

My busy schedule soon took my mind off college, and I turned my attention to preparing my graduation speech. As one of a half-dozen speakers, I had chosen as my topic the founding of the city of Ste. Genevieve, the oldest city west of the Mississippi, which was that year celebrating the two hundredth anniversary of its founding. A detachment of men from Jefferson Barracks, including the Sixth Infantry Band, was to be sent that summer to Ste. Genevieve to participate in the bicentennial pageant. I was fascinated by the history of that city, its relation to the whole of Louisiana, and the struggle of the early settlers with the river which kept changing its course and flooding their houses and fields. I was soon locked up in my room preparing my oration.

I was still involved in debating, and my two debating coaches, Mr. Deming and Mr. Moody, took me aside one afternoon and told me of another scholarship for which they wanted me to apply. Gerard Swope, the president of General Electric and originally from St. Louis, had established a scholarship fund in honor of his parents. The first of the scholarships were to be given that year—three of them to graduates of the St. Louis high schools.

Mr. Deming and Mr. Moody were two of the old-fashioned teachers of the type that made the St. Louis public school system at the time one of the best in the country. Men of intelligence and integrity, they were tireless in their efforts to teach the young and to communicate an enthusiasm for their subjects. With their dark suits and gray hair, they were like two hawks hovering over their nest of young debaters. Mr. Deming, with his sharp birdlike features, glasses, and high-pitched voice, was the more talkative of the two. He seemed always to be restlessly flapping about, trying to help us get this or that point straight, while Mr. Moody, the deeper-voiced and quieter one, would sit brooding in the corner and would break in at crucial moments.

They perched over me one afternoon helping me complete the Swope scholarship application. They knew that I could round up some excellent recommendations from within the school. One of these would come from Miss Gene Meenach, adviser of the senior class. Her sister, Miss Gould Meenach, had been my seventh-grade teacher, and the two sisters had taken a special interest in me all along. They were both enormously plump: Miss Gene, the heavier of

170

the two with light brown hair frizzled out so that she looked like a puffed-up version of Strewelpeter; Miss Gould, jolly and dark. They were both like my maiden aunts, of that selfless breed whose entire lives were given over to their students.

It would be good at the same time, my debating coaches said, to secure some recommendations from outside the school as well. In my case, outside school meant Jefferson Barracks. Who there would be willing to write for me, they asked.

"The Chaplain might," I said.

"That's fine," they said.

"But what about General Short?" asked Mr. Deming.

"Yes, why not General Short?" said Mr. Moody.

They both knew that the general had taken over command of the Barracks the previous year, and that his son Dean was my friend and companion.

I explained that I did indeed know Dean and that I had spoken several times to Mrs. Short, who had been very kind, but that I scarcely knew the general, although he had also been kind. (I was thinking of the suits that he had given me, one of which I was then wearing. I did not mention the suit.)

They decided that they should set out then and there to call on General Short, and ask him for his recommendation. The deadline for turning in the application was upon us, and there was no time to lose.

We were soon in Mr. Deming's car and on the way to Jefferson Barracks. I directed them to General Short's quarters at the middle of Officers' Row. They asked me to wait while they went in.

I looked out across the parade ground and at the barracks beyond. The parade ground was empty now, and in a few minutes retreat would sound. I thought of all the years during which this green expanse had been the focal point of my life with its parades, its picnics, its games. It was like a roll of green Christmas paper in which in my mind I slowly wrapped up my youthful dreams.

Moments passed while my eye followed the men in the distance, toy soldiers now lined up on the edge of the green.

I looked the other way, and behind the dark screen of the porch I saw the red flushed face of General Short. Clad only in a bathrobe, he was shaking hands with his two visitors. Mr. Moody and Mr. Deming were soon back in the car, elated. General Short was ill with influenza, but he had risen from his bed and had typed out a glowing recommendation. We headed back to the North Gate.

The guard at the Gate waved us past, and a few feet beyond we drew up in front of our house. I asked the gentlemen to come in, but I felt my voice tremble as I did. There had been no way to warn my mother of their coming, and heaven knew what they would find. Our bootlegging business had tapered off since Repeal, but there were still a number of old customers who came to drink my father's home brew and whiskey and to share his company. How many of them would we find? But there was something far worse, and I had forgotten about it until I found it staring me straight in the face.

My mother ushered her guests into her dark neat living room. The dining room table was visible through the double door; happily no one was sitting at it. But next to the divanet, directly opposite us as we sat down, stood a slot machine glowing in the semidarkness like a Chinese dragon. My mother was as

172

poised and beautiful as ever and received her guests as graciously as if our house had been an imperial palace and the slot machine beside her a vase of the Ming dynasty.

I could not take my eyes off it and its obscene white metal arm protruding into the darkness. My father had brought the machine home several weeks before. He never said where it came from. I had never seen anyone play it, but there it sat, waiting, I thought in horror, for just this moment.

Mr. Deming and Mr. Moody did not seem to notice the slot machine at all, or if they did they appeared to accept it as the most natural thing in the world to find in a corporal's living room. They left, after having assured my mother that with General Short's recommendation I would receive the scholarship.

My parents were among the crowd that gathered early in the auditorium of Cleveland High School. My mother looked festive in her new outfit of black and white polka dots with a broad-brimmed white straw hat, and my father was neat in his uniform with every button gleaming. Since he almost never went out, I considered it a personal triumph to get him to come. They were soon joined by Mrs. Bradbury, more effusive than ever. She spoke of me as if I were her own son and lectured my parents and all those in the neighboring seats about the glorious development of my voice and pointed to me as an example of the triumph of her method. My mother wondered aloud later that evening whether, in the light of Mrs. Bradbury's assertions, she could herself take credit for anything I had done.

My words on Ste. Genevieve impressed the audience, and people I had never seen before came up afterward to shake my hand. I felt good, but not so good as I would have felt had my name been at the bottom of the program as the recipient of the Washington University scholarship.

Several weeks later on a very hot morning as I sat with twenty other students at Brown's Business School following exercises in the typing manual, the instructor interrupted me to say that I was wanted on the telephone.

It was my father, who said that I had received a notice to appear for an interview for the Swope scholarship at a nearby building within an hour. The notice had been mailed weeks before but had gone to another Smith at Jefferson Barracks and had just come to my father. After we had moved off the post, my father had kept his box at the post office there. Although I received some mail at 9988 South Broadway, I disliked the address. It sounded so completely like the end of the line (exactly what it was, as the last house on a street that followed the river all through St. Louis.) I had also always thought that the Broadway address was a temporary one, and that as soon as my father pulled himself together and became a sergeant again, we would move back to Jefferson Barracks, where we belonged. I was aware also that my military background gave me a clear distinction. In the Swope scholarship application I had been careful to give the Jefferson Barracks address since my sponsors had laid such stress on the recommendation of General Short.

I was shaken to receive the notice so late. There was no time now to go home to get dressed properly, and no time even to collect my wits. Because of the heat, I was in shirt-sleeves, but fortunately my shirt was a clean white one and I was wearing a necktie.

When I reached the waiting room in the office building where the interviews were held, I felt immediately like a pariah. Every boy present was wearing a neatly pressed jacket, and each one looked me up and down with what I took to be a superior, other-side-of-the-tracks air.

We were interviewed by Mr. Horace Swope, the journalist, who had come out from New York, and by Miss Alma Fletcher of the St. Louis Board of Education. They read over some of my poems and stories and asked me questions about my Army background. I was so appalled to be sitting next to them in shirtsleeves that I felt that nothing I said made any sense. I took the long streetcar ride back down Broadway in a state of profound depression.

The next notice came about a week later, and there was no delay in its reaching me. I was one of the three winners of a Swope memorial scholarship, which would cover my tuition and all my expenses at Washington University for four years. A few days later I was notified that I had also received a full scholarship to the University of Missouri. I had completely forgotten that I had taken that spring an examination in history open to high school students throughout the state. I was one of four winners, but my advisers told me to stick with Washington University, and I was delighted to do so.

Miss Alma Fletcher informed me years later that although she and Mr. Swope had been impressed by my record, it was General Short's letter that had won them over completely. I was saying good-bye to the scenes of my childhood, and it seemed fitting that the place that I had known intimately for almost fifteen years had bade me farewell with so generous a gesture.

PART THREE

Having described elsewhere, and in various
ways, what a poet is and having lamented
his status in our society, I have sought in
this book to do the same thing for the soldier, that other pariah of modern times.

— Alfred de Vigny, *The Military
Condition* (*Servitude et Grandeur
Militaires*, 1835), translated by
Marguerite Barnett

14

SAD DAY AT OAHU

Sad day at Oahu
When the Jap beetle hit!
    Our Proustian retort
    Was Kimmel and Short,
Old women in blue,
And then the beetle bit.

—Allen Tate
*Ode to Our Young
Proconsuls of the Air*

Six years later a telephone call that came on the quiet Sunday afternoon of December 7, 1941 cut not only through my nap but like a lightning stroke cut right through my life. I was stretched out on a sofa in the living room of the brick bungalow we then occupied on Telegraph Road, just west of Jefferson Barracks. A classmate at Washington University, where I had received a master's degree in French the previous June, telephoned to tell me that the Japanese had attacked the American fleet at Pearl Harbor.

When I turned on the radio to hear the reports of the Japanese assault on Battleship Row, I had the sensation that the bombs striking there were coming down on us too and were about to blow the bricks of our little bungalow sky high. And, in a sense, they were. The reason was simple: although my mother and I were safe, only a few miles from the military post I had known for most of my life, my father was at Schofield Barracks where the bombs were falling. Or worse, he was perhaps on one of the ships already sunk at Pearl Harbor or in the vicinity of Oahu.

We had had a letter not long before addressed to us from Schofield Barracks, saying that my father's two-year term of duty on Oahu was over and that he would be returning to the States on the fourth of December. We did not have the name of the transport and we did not know whether or not it had sailed, but we assumed that it had.

While my mother sat weeping quietly at the kitchen table, I tried to find out what ships had sailed from Honolulu by calling every possible source of information I could think of, but without success. Another week passed before we found out my father's ship had not sailed and that he was safe at Schofield Barracks.

James Jones has described the scene in which we discovered my father had taken part: "At Schofield Barracks in the infantry quadrangles, those of us who were up were at breakfast. On Sunday mornings in those days there was a bonus ration of a half-pint of milk, to go with your eggs or pancakes and syrup, also Sunday specials. Most of us were more concerned with getting and holding onto our half-pints of milk than with listening to the explosions that began rumbling up toward us from Wheeler Field two miles away.

'They doing some blasting?' some old-timer said through a mouthful of pancakes. It was not till the first low-flying fighter came skidding, whammering low overhead with his MGs going that we ran outside, still clutching our half-pints of milk to keep them from being stolen, aware with a sudden sense of awe that we were being and acting in a genuine moment of history."

My father might well have been the old-timer, asking about the blasting through a mouthful of pancakes, if he had not been in another barracks just down the road, like Jones totally unprepared for what was happening.

As my father later told it, since the sailing of his transport had been delayed, like almost everybody else on Oahu he had been out on the town the night before, but was up early with Jones and the others to enjoy the Sunday specials. The first explosions he took to be blasting or perhaps just another alert; they had had so many in recent weeks. When he went out of his barracks and saw what was happening, he did not linger. In the event of an emergency it was his duty to get his men to the storeroom to pick up their weapons, but since no one was around to unlock the storeroom and since it held no weapons anyway, he decided there was nothing for him to do. And so, while the younger men in his company rushed about like mad roused roosters, he went back calmly into the mess hall and finished his scrambled eggs.

At our kitchen table some four or five thousand miles away, my mother and I were less cool. All the events of my life had prepared me for this afternoon, but I was all the same in a state of shock. As in a speeded-up silent film, the images of my life flickered before my eyes—scenes of marching men on the

181

parade ground, lifted sabers, the flushed face of General Short, now caught so shamelessly by the Japanese, the impassive face of Major Terriagaki, the face of Tommy Reagan smiling against the moonlit backdrop of the rifled fence—and then suddenly the film broke, and I seemed to be staring straight ahead into the white hot bulb of the projector, into the horror of the present. I brought my hand up to my eyes as if to shade them from this present horror and to try to review some of the memories of my college years, now being brought so abruptly to an end.

During my freshman year at Washington University, with our bootlegging days behind us, my mother took a job in the Jefferson Barracks Laundry to help pay the rent. I shared a ride to the University every day with my friend Jack Glascock, a major's son, who had enrolled to take courses until he could get into West Point. He would stop by to pick me up each morning, and then usually in the afternoon because our schedules did not coincide, I would take the long streetcar ride home from the University, transferring several times. Both Jack and I enrolled in R.O.T.C. and I soon got a taste in a small way of what West Point would have been like. It was clear to me that I would never have lasted there. At the end of my first term I was invited to a meeting of the military fraternity, which accepted Jack as a member but turned me down. The fraternity members saw clearly that he was headed for a military career and that I was not.

Toward the end of my freshman year we heard that Boston, the owner of our house at the North Gate, was returning to St. Louis and wanted his house back; we had to find another place. My father was then a frequent customer at Regnier's tavern just beyond the West Gate of the Barracks, and there he learned that a small brick bungalow, owned by Joe Regnier's son, Jo-Jo, was for rent just down the road —on the corner of Sigsbee and Telegraph—which is where we moved and where we found ourselves on December 7, 1941. At the time of our move, we acquired a Model-A Ford—the "Puddle-jumper" or the "Cucaracha," as it was immediately christened— and it was in the driveway when the Japanese struck Pearl Harbor and Schofield Barracks. Ours was a brick bungalow like so many built in the thirties in the area—sturdy, solid, incredibly ugly—four rooms with a cellar, an attic, and a fenced-in yard behind, and a front porch high off the ground, where no one ever sat.

The shift between high school and college is for many students abrupt. For me it was the miraculous crossing of a deep chasm: at times I wanted to destroy the bridge by which I had crossed and to blot out any reminders of my life with the Army. My R.O.T.C. uniform was one such reminder, and I wore it as little as possible; in my sophomore year I hung it up and only occasionally attended class. (I had taken R.O.T.C. in the first place only to avoid taking gym.) Most of my friends at the Barracks had moved away or were soon to leave. Dean Short had gone with his parents to Fort Benning, Georgia, and afterward to West Point. Tommy Reagan had also gone to the Point, and I never saw either of them again. But I still lived on the edge of the Barracks and there were constant reminders that my connection with the military was not over. During my freshman year I still lived in the Boston house, where I slept and studied, perched almost literally above the North Gate of the Barracks. I drove through the post almost every day past all the scenes of my childhood to pick up my mother at the Post Laundry. On Telegraph Road, after we moved, my father would still come home daily with the large sacks of commissaries, and when I returned at night I would sometimes find him at the kitchen table drinking with his fellow Bandsmen. But now more and more his off-duty hours were spent in taverns—at Regnier's at the West Gate or at the Blue Goose, farther out in the country. Regnier's, a few hundred feet from the gate, was a two-story brick structure with a dark high-ceilinged barroom on the ground floor and a large apartment upstairs occupied by Joe Regnier and his family. In the spring and summer there were tables out under the trees behind the building. Presided over by stout and matter-of-fact Joe Regnier (always willing to listen to the soldiers' complaints about the happenings on the post) and his handsome, muscular bartender son, Regnier's was a favorite gathering place for men of the Sixth Infantry. It resembled a good many of the German beer houses and beer gardens in South St. Louis. The Regniers like many of the other inhabitants of the area could probably have traced their ancestry back to the original French settlers of Carondelet's Vide Poche, but now they seemed to have adopted the atmosphere of their German neighbors. All that was needed to give the place a complete feeling of *Gemütlichkeit* was a uniformed brass band pumping away on summer evenings. Even if there was no band, there were numerous Bandsmen without instruments but with plenty of talk. My father became a legendary figure in the establishment. When sometimes in the late afternoon I stopped by to pick him up for dinner, he would introduce me proudly as his son, the college boy. I noticed that my father's stories took precedence

184

over those of the other men at the bar. This was a matter of protocol: deference was shown to old-timers, whatever their rating, even after duty hours. My father became a real hero when one evening he accidentally got locked inside. He went to the bathroom late in the evening, and, heavy with beer, fell asleep and did not come out. So much time went by that Joe Regnier thought that he had gone home, and when closing time came he locked up without checking the bathroom. When my father came to an hour or so later, he tried to find his way through the dark to the door. His stumbling between the tables brought Joe down the stairs with his pistol at the ready. Only my father's familiar snarl kept Joe from firing into the dark at the supposed intruder. The scene, reenacted on both sides of the bar, became a perennial favorite with the customers.

One day during my freshman year I read a notice on a bulletin board at the University about a meeting of the College Poetry Society, to which any interested students were invited. It was to be held at the house of Professor Alexander "Sandy" Buchan of the English Department. When I looked carefully at the address, my eyes almost fell out: Professor Buchan lived on Telegraph Road about a mile from the North Gate of the Barracks. There were no streetlights anywhere in those days along Telegraph Road, and the numbers on the houses were rarely in evidence. I allowed myself ample time, and after a struggle down the dark road, up treacherous driveways, past fierce watchdogs, I found the house and within it a group of friendly young people who were discussing all that I cared most about. The group consisted mainly of bright and pretty girls who all seemed to know one another and who spoke quickly and knowledgeably of many modern writers I had never heard of. They deferred to a young man, older than most of them, who spoke with great authority. He was Clark Mills McBurney, who, as Clark Mills, had already published several poems in national publications. Tall, with sandy hair and an open and friendly manner, he punctuated his sentences with a chuckle that seemed to come from deep within. Several of his poems had been published in *College Verse*, the publication of the College Poetry Society, edited by Ann Winslow from the University of Wyoming.

Miss Winslow, with what appeared to be inexhaustible energy (she must have written hundreds of letters every day to campuses around the country) and a passion for poetry, had organized the College Poetry Society at twenty or thirty major colleges and universities. She raised money for prizes and enlisted the help of established poets to serve as judges for the magazine's annual contests. She had just edited an anthology of selections from *College Verse*, entitled *Trial Balances*. Work of a number of undergraduate poets was presented, accompanied in each case by a critical assessment of the work by a well-known poet. Here Clark's poems were presented with an essay by R.P. Blackmur; Marianne Moore commented on the poems of Elizabeth Bishop. There were other contributions by Theodore Roethke, Josephine Miles, Ben Belitt, and many others who were just beginning to publish. I bought the book immediately, and it became my introduction to modern poetry. And then—urged on by Clark—I started to read T.S. Eliot and the young English poets, Auden, Spender, Day Lewis, and MacNeice.

Clark became my mentor, and I his adoring pupil. He was then a senior at Washington University, and his field was French. He lived in Clayton, not far from the University, and soon invited me to his house, where I spent many hours. On weekends we went together to parties in the suburbs of Webster Groves or Kirkwood at the houses of girls who were students or former students at the University. In these houses, the property usually of well-to-do businessmen, we spent hours reading poetry and listening to music, and I continued to receive the kind of cultural indoctrination that Mrs. Bradbury had begun for me some years before. I now only occasionally visited Mrs. Bradbury's Nautilus Studio since my life was wholly involved with the University.

My meeting with Clark Mills occurred at about the same time as another event that had a lasting effect on my life. Because of my excellent grounding in French, I was placed in an upper section of French composition. I was delighted to learn that there were classes taught by native Frenchmen, and I joined the class of Professor Albert Salvan, who afterward taught at West Point and later became chairman of the French department at Brown University. In the class, conducted in French, we were reading *Le Grand Meaulnes (The Wanderer)* by Alain-Fournier, which I thoroughly enjoyed.

As an assignment early in the semester we were given a list of topics, suggested by the novel, on which we were asked to write. The topic I chose was "Silence." I thought about it for a while without putting a word down on paper, and then just as I was about to start writing, some friends came by and lured me off to the picture show at Jefferson Barracks. We walked to and from the Post Theater over the road from the North Gate where the streetcar track once ran. I can't remember which film we saw, but with all its bright images behind us, we plunged on our return into the woods and were soon surrounded by the mysterious night sounds to which over the years I had become accustomed. The darkness around us seemed unending and the stars above us appeared as close as they must have to those early explorers who made their way down the Mississippi. I thought of the words of Pascal that I had read somewhere: "The eternal silence of those infinite spaces frightens me."

It was late when we got home, but still under the spell of the vast silence of the night through which I had walked, I quickly put down my thoughts on "Silence." When the papers were returned a few days later, I noticed that mine was not among those that Professor Salvan distributed. The next moment I realized that he was holding it in his hand and reading it to the class. At the end of his reading he pronounced my composition of great merit and worthy of a talented French writer, all the more extraordinary to have come from a young American student. He took my essay to Professor Harcourt Brown, who had just come to Washington University as head of the French department, and Professor Brown soon called me to his office. He questioned me about my background and my plans for the future, and asked in which courses I was enrolled. I explained that in addition to English, French, and science, I had enrolled in courses in education, since these were required for a teacher's certificate. High school teaching appeared to be the best I could hope for on graduation. He urged me— commanded me, I felt—to drop the education courses at once and to sign up for courses in French literature, which he gave me special permission to enter. The following week I enrolled in a senior course with Professor Salvan and, with new friends Clark Mills and others, was soon reading Marcel Proust in the original.

Clark Mills came home with me sometimes, but he and a brilliant Mexican classmate, Edgardo Beascoechea, who also became a close friend, were the only college associates who knew anything of my background. The others knew that I came from Jefferson Barracks, but to most of them Jefferson Barracks meant only the photographs of marching men which the St. Louis papers frequently printed.

I was the youngest member of the small circle that gathered around Clark Mills, but I was accepted intellectually and artistically, and that was all that mattered. I developed a new feeling of confidence. I began to put aside my image of myself as a pimply-faced country bumpkin and to take pride in my accomplishments. I saw that it was not necessary to be part of the fraternity/homecoming/prom-oriented section of the student body to feel that I belonged. Indeed I began to think that we in our group were leaders, whatever anyone else thought, either at the University or in the city. St. Louis had produced a number of important writers, even if they had all been recognized only when they had left. I was confident that we too would one day be recognized.

My literary apprenticeship was intensified during my sophomore year by the introduction into our group of another young writer, Thomas Lanier Williams or as he later became known, Tennessee Williams. Tom, who is several years older than I, enrolled at Washington University as a senior. He had already spent several years at the University of Missouri and a disastrous period working in the shoe firm where his father was employed in St. Louis. Clark Mills met him first as a member of Professor Heller's course in modern European literature, where he wrote brilliant papers. The three of us were soon inseparable: we met regularly with the College Poetry Society and sent our poems off to *College Verse*, but we formed an even more closely knit group within the group since we were its most serious members. We met usually at Tom's house on Arundel Place, a few blocks from the University, first in the living room where Mrs. Williams received us, and afterward on the sunporch, where we sat for hours criticizing one another's poems.

I am frequently amused by those who take Tom's autobiographical projection of his family in *The Glass Menagerie* literally and picture him as having inhabited a run-down, seedy old house, if not a downright hovel. The house on Arundel Place, with its Oriental rugs, silver, and comfortable, if not luxurious, furniture,was located in an affluent neighborhood and was higher on the social ladder than Clark Mills' modest house in Clayton. Our entire bungalow on Telegraph Road would have fitted comfortably into one or two of its rooms. Mrs. Williams presided over it as if it were an antebellum mansion. A busy little woman, she never stopped talking, although there was little inflection or warmth in the steady flow of her speech. One topic, no matter how trivial, received the same emphasis as the next, which might be utterly tragic. I had the impression listening to her that the words she pronounced were like the red balls in a game of Chinese checkers, all suddenly released and clicking quickly and aimlessly about the board.

In contrast Tom was the shyest, quietest person I had ever met. His stony-faced silence often put people off: he appeared disdainful of what was going on around him, never joining in the quick give-and-take of a conversation but rather listening carefully and taking it all in. He would sit quietly in a gathering for long periods of time until suddenly like a volcano erupting he would burst out with a high cackle and then with resounding and uncontrollable laughter. Those who knew him well found this trait delightful, but to others it seemed rude and disconcerting. He was certainly quick and ready with words when we discussed our poetry. With one another's efforts we were nothing if not severe. Tom's great god was D.H. Lawrence, and some of his lyrical Laurentian outpourings got cut back in our sessions. Clark's poems had a finish that Tom and I both attempted to emulate, but we raised questions about some of his images and allusions when they did not come through to us. I arrived one evening with a poem about centaurs and what I thought was a powerful treatment of the conflict between head and heart. I still have somewhere my manuscript with Tom's indignant scrawl across the bottom: "Back to the laboratory." And back it went.

Tom's sister, Rose, was rarely mentioned when we came to the house, but we knew that she was up in her room, perhaps listening at the top of the stairs. Rose was soon to undergo a prefrontal lobotomy, which would be of little help to her. Clark saw much more of Rose during the following summer, while I was away in Michigan on a summer job, so much more indeed that he appears to be the prototype of the Gentleman Caller in *The Glass Menagerie*. That summer Clark and Tom set up in Clark's basement what they called a literary factory. They were visited, Tom said later in an introduction of his poems, by Clark's mother—bringing them chocolate and cookies—more often than by the muse.

At the end of that summer Clark went to Paris to study at the Sorbonne on a fellowship provided by the University, and his parting left a gap in our little group. But Tom and I went on with our literary endeavors. Continuing to meet regularly on Arundel Place, we were soon joined by Louise Krause, who had attended Mills College in California and had come back home to St. Louis to take a master's degree in English at the University. Louise, when not busy with her thesis on John Donne, composed metaphysical poems that impressed Tom and me. The three of us formed what we called "The St. Louis Poets Workshop." We were joined by Elizabeth Fenwick Phillips, who later married Clark Mills and as Elizabeth Fenwick wrote several fine mystery novels. We had some stationery printed with the words "St. Louis Poets Workshop" as the letterhead and Tom's address below. We sent poems to all the leading magazines with a covering letter signed by a fictitious secretary of the workshop. In a few carefully chosen words the letter described the great poetic flowering then taking place in St. Louis. The poems enclosed, the secretary stated, were representative samples of this remarkable Midwestern Renaissance. The editors addressed were less impressed by our flowering than we were: the poems all came back. I had forgotten all about the St. Louis Poets Workshop until one day five years later on Palmyra Island in the Pacific I received a letter from my father written on the Workshop paper that he had found somewhere on my desk. Perhaps it was his way of reminding me of the foolish things that I had put behind me since becoming a responsible Naval officer.

While Tom at the time wrote chiefly poetry, he had already written at least one play, and as a member of Professor William G. B. Carson's playwriting course, he had embarked on others. Clark and I listened one evening to a reading of his play "Ishtar," a Babylonian bedroom saga. Tom intended it as a deadly serious drama, but the language and the situations that it presented were so absurd that we doubled up with laughter. It also went back to the laboratory and was never mentioned again.

Tom's next involvement with the theater was as an actor in a French-language production of Molière's *Les Fourberies de Scapin* put on by the University's French department. Mrs. Harcourt Brown, the wife of the French department chairman, had a passion for theater and a determination to present French drama, however difficult the casting and however varied the French accents of the actors she rounded up. Edgardo Beascoechea, Thelma Richardson, and I had acted in one of Mrs. Brown's first efforts, *La Bataille des Dames*, but that was a modest effort beside *Scapin*. We were again enlisted, and Tom was persuaded to take the part of the old father. He read his French lines with a kind of hound-dog ferocity and deliberation, as if he were chewing on a large section of the Mississippi delta. When he moved woodenly across the stage with absolute seriousness pounding the floor with his cane, small and square in his satin suit, an enormous blond wig flopping about on his shoulders, he gave a performance that a more sophisticated audience would have taken as deliberate high camp. As it was, our local audience had not the remotest idea of when to laugh since it had not a clue as to what was going on.

Tom's theatrical involvement soon took a more serious turn. For the annual competition in Professor Carson's drama course, he wrote a one-act play entitled "Me, Vasha." The play concerns a munitions-maker and his mad wife. Vasha was the first of Tom's many splendid, wild heroines. I thought at the time that the play was superb, but my opinion was not shared by the judges of the competition. "Me, Vasha" was not one of the plays chosen for presentation. It was rejected in favor of a bit of fluff by one of Professor Carson's protégés. Those of us around Tom were outraged. This rejection had much to do with souring him on Washington University and sending him off the following year to the University of Iowa.

On the day of the Japanese attack, all my undergraduate years—the scenes of joyous friendship, youthful triumphs and disappointments—passed before my eyes. I thought of commencement day two years before in June 1939 when, in the Field House of Washington University—where I had first gone as a member of the Cleveland High School chorus—I received my B.A. degree. For me it was a great day, but for my mother it was a day when her joy and pride and sense of fulfillment knew no bounds: I was the first member of my family on either side to graduate from college. All her sacrifices had been worth it: for her the diploma was more than just a sheet of paper. It was positive proof that from the beginning she had been right to encourage me in all my work, even when, as with my poetry, she did not always fully grasp what I was doing.

She was beaming as we gathered in front of the brick bungalow on Telegraph Road.

"Now, let *me* try it on," my mother said, after photographing me in my cap and gown.

And she put on the cap and gown and held the diploma in her hands as if it were a sacred scroll.

"Now it's my turn," said Aunt Lucinda, as dark and plump as ever.

"And now, mine," said my cousin Erminie, tall, thin, and beautiful. They had both come over from East St. Louis for the day.

There was no end to the laughter and high spirits. It felt good to have their approval and to have them share this day.

Conversation rippled on while my mother laid out a delicious luncheon of fried chicken, a rich assortment of vegetables, and corn bread.

When we went in to the table, I draped the gown over an armchair, its wide black sleeves hanging down like the wings of a fallen bird.

I had a fleeting sense, as we ate, of the dark gown, a kind of shadow that hovered over our joy. For however joyous the occasion, it was obvious to all that one important person was absent from the table. It had been my father's luck to draw guard duty at the West Gate of the Barracks that day, and a picture of him waving the cars on flashed through my mind. Aunt Lucinda's laughter became more and more insistent, taking on an hysterical edge as it moved in to cover my father's absence. I could see him waving the cars past more quickly, his arms flailing in the air like wounded wings. No one needed to tell me that he was drunk.

That evening after Aunt Lucinda and Erminie had left, word reached us that he had had his belt pulled and was in the guardhouse. This time his negligence had been too blatant to be passed over. My day of triumph may have made him sense all the more acutely his own past failures. Or was it sheer cussedness or some inner torment that even he could not understand that led him to lose all control on this particular day? He never spoke to me of it afterward, and I never knew. He was busted, and to spare his family further embarrassment, he was allowed to transfer to another base. It was thus that he had joined General Short at Schofield Barracks in Hawaii, where he was eating scrambled eggs on the morning of December 7, 1941, when the Japanese planes swooped down.

15

DEATH OF THE CORPORAL

"*Hup* - two - three - four! *Hup* - two - three - four!"

The sounds were familiar, and I'd been here before, but how different it all was now!

The time was February 1942, and I was marching not in khaki on the green parade ground of my boyhood but in the navy blue of a reserve cadet. The place was the Near North Side of Chicago on the edge of Lake Michigan, only a mile or two from where I had shared my father's tent at the Century of Progress Exposition almost ten years before. I had enlisted in the V-2 Officers Training Program, and in a few months would receive my commission as an ensign in the U.S. Naval Reserve and be assigned to regular duty.

I was one of the "ninety-day wonders." At the moment with the ice wind whipping off the lake and slapping my face, the cold of the snow-bound walks biting at my legs like a mastiff as I marched, the experience seemed anything but wonderful.

The previous June, on the day I received my

master of arts in French from Washington University, I also received a notice from my draft board. The graduate schools of both Johns Hopkins and Princeton had offered me fellowships to continue work toward a Ph.D., but there could be no deferral to take them up.

I did not want the military life in any form, but since it was being forced on me, I chose what seemed the lesser of two evils. In the Navy I would be making use of my college background and within a few months drawing an officer's pay. Financial considerations were a major concern: for the previous two years I had been an Assistant in French, teaching classes in beginning and intermediate French and helping my mother with the expenses of our house on Telegraph Road. An ensign's pay would be of more help, and she would perhaps be able to give up her job in the Barracks Laundry. I had met all the requirements for enlistment in the V-2 program except for a course in trigonometry, which I had completed the previous summer. I was underweight, and had continued to be until the day of my physical in the fall. I went to my girlfriend's house for lunch and, after a large meal, I ate as many bananas and drank as many steins of beer as I could hold. I weighed in at just over the minimum required. I was then accepted in the program, and while waiting to be called, I took a job typing manifests for a trucking company on the St. Louis waterfront.

With the Japanese attack, I was one of thousands of young men marching to the defense of the country.

"*Hup* - two - three - four! *Hup* - two - three - four!"

We were on our way from the Armory, where we drilled each morning, to Abbott Hall, the lakeshore high-rise dormitory of Northwestern University,

198

which served as our training ship. I shared one of the small rooms with John McCormick, a lean, solemn-appearing but witty graduate student in English from Minneapolis, and Hubert Dawkins, a dark, plump, jovial, balding Georgian. McCormick was an admirer of Robert Frost, and in the few spare moments that we had he would bring out Frost's latest volume. Dawkins had some twenty or so small bottles of various substances—liquids and pomades—which he applied morning and night to his hair. All these had to be whisked up and out of sight within a minute or two. Our door had to be kept open at all times and the room immaculate, the blankets on the bunks squared away, the desks free of debris. Our room, particularly, had to be kept in order since it was opposite that of Capt. Wintergate Bingham, the commanding officer of our lakeshore training ship.

Captain Bingham seemed a movie version of a Naval officer. Gray and distinguished looking, ram-rod straight in his immaculate dark blue uniform, he tolerated no nonsense, and when he addressed us "young gentlemen," he admonished us always to be disciplined and observant.

"Mate of the deck!" he called out one day.

Jim Riley, a young Irish-American on duty at the time, whipped down the hall into the door, clicked his heels, and saluted.

"Mate of the deck," Captain Bingham growled, "there's too much noise out there on the deck."

"Some of the men have been missing muster, sir," Riley replied.

And then he paused.

"Besides, sir..." He paused again, intensifying his gaze, his bright eyes clicking. "If I may say so, sir, the flagpole needs painting."

Taken aback, Captain Bingham wheeled around and gazed out at the flagpole.

"Right you are, young man," he snapped. "I can see that you've learned to use your eyes."

The next day men were out painting the flagpole.

We soon learned that it was appropriate for Captain Bingham to stress the necessity of being observant. He himself had learned the price of not being so when, a few years previously, the cruiser that he commanded ended up on rocks off the California coast. He had been summarily retired from service until the Japanese attack had brought him back to regular duty.

"*Hup* - two - three - four!"

As the cold bit at my legs, I thought of how the war had been closing in on me since the summer of 1938. With money that I saved from odd jobs during the previous two years, I had gone to study in France at the Institut de Touraine in Tours. In Paris I had a happy reunion with Clark Mills, who was about to return to teach at Cornell. I came back in September on the *De Grasse*, and I could recall the near panic on board among the French crew at the time of the Munich crisis. The day we reached the New York harbor there was the worst fog in years. The crossing was rough, but fortunately I discovered that I had good sea legs. The third-class cabins around me on the *De Grasse* were packed with refugees, mostly from Nazi Germany, and some of them had been so sick in the final days that they could not move from the passageways. I had to step over them on the way up to the deck, where I spent most of the time. But when we reached New York, we all had to remain below because of the thick fog; the ship inched ahead, the fog horn sounding incessantly. We were allowed back

200

on deck as the New York skyline poked at us through holes in the fog and the torch of Liberty seemed wreathed in cotton gauze. I will never forget the dark, steady gaze of the sick refugees who lined the railings, trying to make out the gray buildings ahead. Nor will I ever forget the dark gaze of the members of the Lincoln Brigade on board, who had fought for the Spanish Republic, when the Immigration Officers brutally removed their passports. They had volunteered to fight against a Fascist dictatorship in a terrible war that was but the forerunner of a greater war. A few years later, along with the others of us, those who were fleeing to America and those who had fled long before, they would be marching again when war spread round the world.

"*Hup* - two - three - four!"

I enjoyed some of the required courses at Abbott Hall, such as those in navigation, but most of the time I took in the information that was piled upon us and simply fed it back mechanically on the regular quizzes. My mind and body were being disciplined like machines and only on Saturday afternoon and evening, when we were allowed out for liberty, would they relax. Sometimes the machines would falter, and I wondered if I was going to be able to make it through the training period. Close order drill was particularly trying. My roommate McCormick marched in front of me, and twice on the way back from the Armory on the cold mornings I had swung my foot too far forward and had caught the back of his rubber and caused it to come loose from his shoe. This morning the wind whipped in from the lake, my mind wandered, my foot again came down on McCormick's rubber, cutting it loose again. Now, rather than reaching down to adjust it and without losing a step, he

201

raised his foot in perfect time, high in the air, and kicked the loosened rubber into a snow drift. He continued without it to Abbott Hall.

My prowess in close order drill did not improve, but I managed to drag through, something less than a wonder, and, along with my commission in May, I received orders to report to Pearl Harbor.

During spare moments on weekends I had completed two short poems, and a few weeks before the end of training I had sent them to *Poetry*, the Chicago magazine of verse, then located on East Erie Street, two or three blocks from Abbott Hall. I had sent poems for years to *Poetry*, which was founded by Harriet Monroe in 1912 and published the early work of T.S. Eliot, Wallace Stevens, and others. My early submissions had all been rejected, but this time an acceptance came back from the editor George Dillon, and with it an invitation to visit the office. So a few days after commissioning I read my poems to a group of Chicago poets George Dillon had gathered together in his office. I stood in my bright new Naval uniform while the faces of former contributors stared down from photographs lining the walls. Many of them had put on uniforms in World War I, and some had not returned.

A few weeks later I sat with my father at the Halekulani Hotel in Waikiki. I went out to see him at Schofield Barracks just after my arrival in Hawaii, and he had come to spend the weekend with me at the Beach Walk Inn, around the corner from the Halekulani, where I lived while working as a communications officer at a headquarters hidden away in the mountains. He was happy and proud to see me, and I introduced him proudly to several of my officer colleagues who lived in the elegant cabins of the Halekulani, which had been taken over by the Navy.

While sun filtered down through the palm trees and mynah birds paraded across the trim lawns and breakers pounded the white sand, we sat on a screened-in porch drinking beer. My father regaled my fellow officers with a long account of the Japanese attack, ending up with the picture of himself eating scrambled eggs while the planes swept down.

Drinking had earned him a stay in the infamous stockade at Schofield Barracks, but he did not speak of that now. He was again wearing his corporal's chevrons.

His regiment was scheduled to depart soon for the South Pacific, and he was determined not to go with it.

"But how can you avoid it?" I asked.

"My heart condition," he said.

I looked astonished; I had never heard of a heart condition.

"I'll get out," he continued, a determined look on his face. "I'm not going down there in the jungle with those guys."

When I left Oahu a few months later, assigned as communications and afterward personnel officer on Palmyra Island, a thousand miles southwest of Honolulu, my father left also to return to the States. Not all the doctors apparently believed that he had serious heart trouble, but he convinced enough of them that he had to get his retirement. If he had waited another three years and resumed his sergeant's rating, his retirement pay would have been much higher. But he wanted out; he had seen enough.

The yeoman who worked with me at the Palmyra Air Base pointed out one day that, according to Navy regulations, qualified officers should report their language ability each year. I wrote a letter to Washington, giving my entire background in French, Italian, and Spanish, and requesting that I be transferred where one or another of these languages might be useful. I had forgotten all about the letter when months later orders came through that took me from Palmyra to Casablanca. After some months ashore I replaced a Britisher as liaison officer on board the French Sloop *La Grandière*, a ship resembling an American gunboat, which had been built before the war as a patrol vessel for the French colonies. I went first with the *La Grandière* to Norfolk, where it was refitted as an escort vessel, and then sailed with it to join the South Pacific Fleet. Although we had three five-inch guns, we lacked speed, and were usually left behind when other ships moved forward. For many months we were a station ship at Tulagi, opposite Guadalcanal, at Espiritu Santo in the New Hebrides, and at Funafuti, thousands of miles from anywhere. I had only two close calls during my year and a half on board. We had been tied up for some days next to an ammunition ship at Guadalcanal. We received orders unexpectedly to sail at dawn to escort a cargo vessel to Manus Island, a staging area for the fleet preparing for the Battle of Leyte. A few hours after we sailed the ammunition ship blew up and with it the entire dock at Guadalcanal. (My father was right that Guadalcanal, where his regiment had been headed from Schofield Barracks, was not the best place to be.) On another occasion at Espiritu Santo I had gone on board a training submarine on its daily run outside the harbor. I was standing with the commanding officer on the conning tower when he spotted an American plane, which, taking us for an enemy sub, was zooming down on us. In seconds the commanding officer

got the submarine far enough below the surface so
that, although badly damaged by the bombs the plane
dropped, and shaken like a cocktail shaker, we were
able to make it back to port. That was my first and last
journey on a submarine.

Most of the time there was little for me, and my
liaison party of three French-Canadians from New
England, Jean-Paul Tanguay, Francis Morrissey, and
Louis Contois, to do but to decode messages and act
as interpreters. We all had a good many pleasant
moments aboard what the American officers in the
South Pacific referred to as "the floating cocktail
lounge," because, unlike American ships, the *La
Grandière* carried wine and liquor on board.

When I returned to St. Louis for a brief time after
the war, I found that my mother had moved again, to
another small house in Lemay. She had become
manager of the Barracks Laundry during the war, and
had supervised the work of scores of German prisoners. Later she had transferred to the Veterans Hospital adjacent to the Barracks, where she worked as a
telephone receptionist. My father continued to spend
most of his time at taverns, at Regnier's and the Blue
Goose. The tension between my parents had increased
over the years, and they were divorced soon after I left
St. Louis for good. My mother then transferred to a
Veterans Hospital in Long Beach, California. She
remarried some years later, gave up her job, and
enjoyed life on a lovely, quiet street in Long Beach,
not far from Sergeant O'Hara and other retired non-
coms from Jefferson Barracks. My father took a job as
a guard at a government building and lived in a small
hotel in St. Louis. He left that job to join his brother
George on Saline Lake in Winnfield, Louisiana, but
the two could not get along, and my father then moved

205

to California, first to Gardena, where he was a frequent visitor to the poker clubs, and then to San Diego, where he seldom left his small room.

When I went to visit my father in San Diego with my two young sons, he always had a hundred dollar bill waiting for me on the edge of the table.

My sons were delighted by my father's wry humor and his strange way of life. He sat most of the day facing the wall, turning his small radio on only once or twice a day for news broadcasts. When it was warm, he fanned himself with a fan fashioned from a large box of cornflakes. In the corner of his bare room, upside down in a shoe box, rested an old alarm clock.

"Why is the clock upside down?" my sons asked.

"That's the only way I can get it to work."

And that is how it stayed for years.

His life continued in this fashion until one day when he started hearing voices in the wall. He called my mother, who went to get him and moved him to Porterville in central California, where he lived in a small hotel near my brother and his wife. When my brother moved his sign business from his ranch on the edge of town, my father went there and stayed in the house to protect it from marauders. He was there, his only companion a dachshund bitch that had arrived one day on his doorstep, when I saw him for the last time. The dachshund died giving birth a little later, and when the ranch was sold, my father moved back to town. When he complained of not feeling well, my sister-in-law took him to the Veterans Hospital. The doctors there wanted to keep him, but he insisted on returning to his hotel. He died a few weeks later of a heart attack when he walked out one morning to have breakfast. It was June 7, 1974, exactly one month before his eighty-third birthday.

Death of the Corporal

Porterville in the San Joaquin Valley in central California at the foot of the Sierra Nevada Mountains is a town of some 20,000 people, many of them the Okies who settled there at the time of the Dust Bowl in the thirties. The town sent more men to fight in the Vietnam War than any town of comparable size in the country. We laid my father to rest among the graves of some of those young men in a beautiful cemetery on the edge of town with a wide sweep of the Sierra Nevada Mountains in the distance.

The burial, arranged by the Tulare County Veterans Council of Foreign Wars, was a proper military one. My father, who told me many times that when you die you are nothing but trash, would have roared with laughter at the comic aspects of his burial. The bugler was clearly better at whatever else in life he did than bugle: the notes of the taps he sounded over the grave wound off through the bright sunlight toward the snowy crests like the steps of a soldier stumbling upstairs through the dark. The bespectacled, scrawny V.F.W. member who read the service spoke with a heavy German accent. Listening to him, I thought of my father as we had seen him earlier laid out in the coffin in his trim black suit, his face as calm and white as the mountain snow. His right hand, with which he had tried to stop his fall to the pavement when his heart attack had come, was dark blue and black. It was as if he had given one final blow in his struggle with life; he had lost, but he had gone out fighting.

Hearing my father's name pronounced in the heavily German-accented English, I thought of an incident that was said to have occurred in the early days of Jefferson Barracks. Old "Blood and Guts," Zachary Taylor, who had himself come up, bowlegged and abrupt, through the ranks, was inspecting the troops. One of his favorite methods of getting his men into shape was what was called "wooling," which meant an officer's pulling on a soldier's ear as he gave him hell. General Taylor stopped to "wool" one of the men whose uniform was in disarray, and the man, a German immigrant who understood little English and was not sure what was going on, swung at Taylor and knocked him to the ground. When the company commander started to rush the man off to the guardhouse, Taylor got to his feet, stopped him and said, "Leave that man alone; he will make a good soldier."

My father, the corporal who had struck his final blow at life, had also been a good soldier. The Army he served would never again be the same; it would never again be the big family that both he and I had known. The Army was losing its human dimension, and would be the poorer for it. The old non-commissioned officers like my father, who had whipped their men into shape whatever their own failings, had no place in the new volunteer Army. Their places were being taken by younger men—and now, of course, by younger women as well—who would be better trained and who would have better pay and more authority. When it came to the business of fighting a war, the Vietnam War had shown it was not the enlisted men who cheated in serious matters like body counts, but their officers who forgot all about honor when it came to making themselves look good. Zachary Taylor said that "unless practice can be blended with theory, the latter will be of little service." What this would mean in the future surely was the upgrading of the practical well-trained enlisted men and women and the downgrading of the theoretical and abstract-minded officers turned out by the United States Military Academy.

Or it may be that my father had not wanted to be a soldier at all but rather an artist, and that his happiest moments had been when he played his clarinet. Having failed as an artist, he had settled for the Army, where failure could not be tolerated and where the order that art demands from within is imposed from without. I had perhaps learned from him not how to be a soldier but how to be an artist. However much one believes in democracy as a form of government, in art, as in the military, all are not equal, and poor performance, whatever one's rank, can never be rewarded. Like the soldier, that other pariah, the artist develops a tough skin, accepting a hard life and at times the scorn of a society that must in the end turn to him for its defense. And society ultimately rewards the artist for his gift, for his ability to transform the lost battles and agonies and sufferings of life into enduring triumphs.

My father left me a thousand dollars. Among his papers, I found the fan made of the cornflakes box, some photographs of Jefferson Barracks (reproduced here for the first time), and an article on the Old Soldiers Home. On brown commissary wrapping paper he had described with great care a method for finding the square root of a number. There was also a list of aphorisms that he had clipped from a newspaper. At the bottom of the list he had added several of his own; the final one was:

> Clear thinking is usually followed by a good bowel movement; most people are terribly constipated.

16

THE BIVOUAC OF THE DEAD

On a rainy day in November of 1977 I returned to Jefferson Barracks. I found my way to South Broadway, up and down which I had traveled so many times in a yellow clanging streetcar, watching, between the old brick buildings, the muddy river flowing a few blocks away. Now stretching along the river from downtown St. Louis to Lemay and the beginnings of Jefferson Barracks was a huge industrial complex, one plant after another. With their array of chimneys, white metal tubes, and tanks, the plants resembled the gloved hands of automatons reaching up into the sky and out over the water. Farther down, as I gazed on the houses I had known and occupied as a boy, I became aware more than ever before of the two inventions that have completely transformed our lives within a quarter of a century: air-conditioning and television. Almost all the porches of the wooden bungalows where people once sat conversing in swings on hot summer evenings were now enclosed, sealed in, often with fake brick-red and purple tar paper, their windows fitted with air-conditioning units, their roofs topped by TV aerials like the ribs of huge umbrellas stripped and flattened by storms. The Boston house, the center of our bootlegging establishment, was covered with large panels of bright red aluminum siding. The trees around it had been cut down and the back yard leveled: the grape arbor, the shrubs, the flowers had all disappeared. The white limestone gates to Jefferson Barracks with their black cannon balls, without the guardhouse or any buildings beside them, looked like the abandoned section of a stage set or the entrance to oblivion in a painting by Magritte. The northern section of the Barracks was now a park and belonged to St. Louis County.

I turned off just past the gates toward the limestone buildings, the oldest on the post. Two of them had been carefully restored, one as a museum, and the other, originally the laborers' house, furnished with period furniture. All the photographs, newspapers, uniforms, weapons, and other materials relating to the Barracks had been carefully assembled in the museum. The dioramas with manikins in the uniforms of the different periods through which the post had passed were all done with attention to the most minute detail. But I felt slightly ill after I examined them all and went out to stand on the terrace opposite the building, from which I gazed on a broad sweep of the Mississippi. How alive the Barracks was in my memory and how dead it seemed here! I might just as well have been visiting a display from the tombs of ancient Egypt, for all that this had to do with me.

I felt the dead eyes of the uniformed manikins follow me along as I drove on toward the heart of the Barracks, which is now occupied by the Air Force Reserve. The grounds under the oak trees had been

211

cleared of all underbrush, and the sinkholes filled in. I paused for a moment before the gate to the house once occupied by General Kress. The house had been demolished, and many of the black rifle barrels from the Civil War in the surrounding fence had been removed. I drove on toward the parade ground. The barracks around it were exactly as they had been, but the officers' quarters, facing them, looked like abandoned tenements. The county had allowed them to serve as public housing when the Barracks had been deactivated, and they were now in a sorry state. The parade ground was enclosed by a high fence and in the middle of it was a mass of what I took to be wind and weather instruments. It was fitting perhaps that the instruments should be here where Albert Berry made the first parachute jump in history, but it was also a strange irony that in the gray mist the whole assembly evoked the remains of a wrecked dirigible, the emblematic skeleton left behind when the spirit of the place had flown.

I drove up to Headquarters Building and paused again beside the dark brooding Spanish cannon; the sundial beside it had disappeared. I gazed down at the railroad station below, boarded up now, at the track where no trains passed, and toward the river beyond. I drove behind Officers' Row, turned up toward the Hospital, which is now a school, circled around behind the Movie Theater, and came out on the Western Front. To the right, where the old cantonment buildings had stood, were row after row of subdivision houses (part of the land in this area had been sold for private housing), as alike one another as the original quarters had been but without any space around them. To the left as far as I could see were the white crosses of graves. The Cemetery, which had originally occupied a small space on a bluff beside the river, had gradually moved west. The field where the tents of the Civilian Military Training Corps had been pitched during the summers, and where I had wandered up and down selling popcorn, was now completely covered by graves.

At the far end of what had been the Western Front, I parked across from the entrance to the Cemetery. The stone gates, emblazoned with a large black eagle and bearing in solid black the letters U.S. NATIONAL CEMETERY, stood exactly where the K.C. Building, my first residence in the Barracks, had been. In the wooded area to the right of the gate, I watched as a yellow bulldozer tore up the ground, making way for more graves. The Cemetery was now the second largest military cemetery in the nation, and it would go on expanding until it covered all the remaining wooded land of what had once been Jefferson Barracks.

I got out of my car and took a few steps, looking neither right nor left but rather down at my feet. The only familiar thing was the sidewalk on which I was standing, and I started down it as I had many times long ago. I examined every bit of it, carefully stepping over the cracks as I had as a boy. Two-thirds of the way down, at a point where the last cantonment building had stood and where the bayonet course had begun, the sidewalk stopped abruptly, its final section tilted up in the air by the roots of a maple tree. I looked up and across the street, now known as Memorial Drive: there as far as I could see stretched the white crosses of the graves. Through the wet gray air their long lines reached toward me, thin bony fingers like the ribs of a ghostly fan extending as if through time. I thought of the lines of Lt. Theodore O'Hara, who was once a member of the Sixth Infantry and had been brevetted for gallantry in Mexico. He later served as aide to Col. Sidney Johnson of the Confederate forces when Johnson was killed at the battle of Shiloh. In tribute to the dead in the Mexican War he had written:

> On Fame's eternal camping ground
> Their silent tents are spread
> And glory guard with solemn round
> The bivouac of the dead.

I walked back up the sidewalk and through the Cemetery gates. In front of the Administration building the members of a black family, who had just come from the stretch of temporary gravesites across the way, were removing the mud from their shoes as they got into their car. Inside, another black family was asking the directions to one of the graves, and the young man at the desk was showing on the numbered grid how to find it. I picked up the brochure that presented the Cemetery's history.

The first interment in the plot of land set aside for the purpose was believed to have been in 1827. The burial ground had been enlarged in 1863 to provide places for the Union soldiers who died in the St. Louis area. The Cemetery became a national one in 1866 under the authority of a joint resolution of the Senate and House of Representatives. Here are the graves of more than 12,000 Union dead and of some 1,140 Confederate dead, many of whom died at St. Louis while prisoners of war. Within the graveyard are other graves containing the remains of 3,255 other unidentified members of the Armed Forces—"known but to God." In addition to the graves of participants

214

in World Wars I and II, there are others of those who had fought in the Mexican War, the Spanish-American War, the Philippine Insurrection, Korea, Vietnam, and, of course, the Indian Wars.

Private Richard Gentry of Virginia, a soldier in the Revolutionary War, is also buried here, his white marble headstone inscribed with the words: "Present at the Capture of Cornwallis at Yorktown." Among the other graves, which the Cemetery brochure does not mention, is that of Mrs. Barbara A. Oswald, who had served in the United States Army from 1967 to 1975. She was buried on Memorial Day, 1977, with full military honors including a twenty-one gun salute —three rifle volleys fired by a squad of seven soldiers in full dress—all in spite of the circumstances of her death. She was killed attempting to highjack a helicopter which she had rented in St. Louis for the purpose of flying to the Marion, Illinois, penitentiary to aid in the escape of two convicts. Like some Vietnam War veterans who had returned to civilian life as drug addicts or outlaws, she had died a criminal, but she had served her country as a good soldier and had earned her place among the honored dead.

I walked over the muddy ground and inspected some of the recent graves, heaped with wreaths and garlands of wilting flowers. The temporary grave markers read: Weyerman, Melvin, U.S. Navy; Wilson, Johnny, Private, U.S. Army...and on and on. I thought of Tommy Reagan, my boyhood friend, a West Point graduate who had been killed in North Africa in World War II, and of my young cousin Odell Nash, a private in the Marine Corps, who had died in the Philippines when the Japanese attacked in 1941. I walked back through the Cemetery gate, marked on the inner side with the large black letters:

215

PEACE. The bulldozer with its yellow snout was roaring through the mud and uprooting more and more trees as I drove down the hill. I turned at the bottom into what is now the Sylvan Springs Park Area. A natural amphitheater, through which the spring trickles, it is now a gathering place for picnickers, and clearly less carefully policed than it was in the thirties when the officers of the Sixth Infantry held their hunt breakfasts here. The amphitheater was empty now, and I sped past the detritus of the picnickers, to the spring itself. I parked beside it, my heart beating faster, as if I were rushing to greet a great love I had not seen for many years. I remembered having lain here beside the spring for hours as a boy, while it flowed, cold and clear, through my fingers, a long white scarf enveloping its jeweled pebbles. And I remembered touching it gently with my lips and drinking in great gulps a cold, pure, silken liquid that seemed to come from the naked heart of the earth. Now I stepped down the concrete steps that enclosed the spring: on each side the mason had let his fancy have free reign and had fashioned in the cement a relief of smiling squirrels eating nuts; in the middle of the steps in swirling letters was inscribed: SYLVAN SPRINGS. It was a monument of pure kitsch, a tribute in the worst possible taste to the spirit of the place. Below me, under a series of arched, concrete, Japanese-y bridges, I found the spring, now a thread of thick green scum choked with brown oak leaves. I raised my eyes to the spot where the water like bile oozed from the hillside. Above it stood a wooden sign: WARNING—UNSAFE WATER—DO NOT DRINK—STATE BOARD OF HEALTH. I gazed up beyond it, through the wet oaks, at the houses of the adjoining subdivision.

216

The Bivouac of the Dead

I walked back to my car and drove out of the park, through the West Gate of the Barracks, and onto Telegraph Road. It was getting dark as I looped back eastward and soon crossed the Mississippi to the broad farmland of southern Illinois, which had sent so many of the men I had known in the twenties and thirties to Jefferson Barracks, many of whom now rested there within their graves.

As I drove on into the dark, I felt the long, bony hand from that bivouac of the dead reaching into the night and heard the sound of taps ringing in my ears. Where indeed was the grandeur of the military condition, of which the poet Alfred de Vigny had spoken? Was that condition ever anything but the pure servitude, of which he had also spoken? What, I asked myself, was the point of the deaths of so many men and women in so many wars, just or unjust, if we now made war on the earth itself and befouled its beauty that had so benefitted us? Was our modern Army, more and more mechanized, more and more inhuman, meant only to carry a message of destruction farther and farther across the earth and on into space? Had I returned to the scenes of my boyhood only to gaze upon the emblematic presentation of this final desecration?

It was dark now and my headlights cut through wisps of fog; I might have been in the middle of nowhere. I realized suddenly that I was not far from another much older graveyard that I had visited the day before. This was at Cahokia, Illinois, directly across from St. Louis, where, within a few miles of the shining Saarinen arch, on the edge of the highway, surrounded by block after block of honky-tonks and shabby buildings, lies a bit of park enclosing the most remarkable Indian burial mounds in the United States.

On this site, at the junction of rivers in what is known as the American Bottomlands, archaeological excavations have recently established that there flourished between 900 and 1300 A.D. an important community of some 30,000 people in the midst of the wilderness (no bigger city existed on the North American continent until Philadelphia grew to that size in 1800). This community had extensive and important trading connections with a third of the continent. In its heyday it covered six and a half square miles and had more than one hundred mounds, the highest of which, the largest such structure in the United States, is a hundred feet high, covers sixteen acres, and contains about 22 million cubic feet of earth. While similar to the ziggurats of Babylon and the pyramids of the Incas, these mounds were entirely the work of North American Indians. Why the community disappeared is not known. In some of the graves that the mounds contain have been discovered copper, mica, conch-shell beads, and arrowheads, all indicative of an affluent society, along with the rounded stones used in a gambling game that was still being played by Choctaw Indians in the mid-nineteenth century.

In my mind's eye as I drove on I pictured a scene that is supposed to have taken place there regularly in prehistoric times. Late in July at dawn the paramount chief of the tribe, representing the Great Sun in a cape of shell beads and a high crown of feathers, kneels to greet the sun at the top of the pyramid. A cry goes up from the crowd of thousands in the forty-acre square below, as a tattooed warrior, face painted red, carries in a bowl the red-hot embers of the eternal fire that is kept burning in the inner temple antechamber of the pyramid. The warrior slowly descends and empties the bowl in the center of the plaza into a pile of leaves and branches at the heart of a cross made of logs pointed in the four cardinal directions. Flames leap up from the cross, a fresh fire annually renewed for the harvest festival, brought down from the heavens, a gift of the sun itself.

Now returning to these American Bottomlands, to the scenes of my boyhood, the heart of my country and the depth of myself, I felt that I had somehow been touched by that ancient fire. It was perhaps to attempt to rekindle it and distill a bit of the land's original essence that I had come back. In learning about my own life and its origins, I had learned something of the nature of conquest, of the conquering and the conquered, and of the land that conquers all. That knowledge and the thought that I might be but the smallest part of a great mysterious whole filled me with a strange joy as I moved slowly on into the night, on toward the east from which I had come.

NOTE

To the best of my knowledge, all the events in this chronicle took place as I have described them, but I have changed the names of a few people when I felt they might in any way be offended by what I have related. Those whose real names remain will understand, I trust, that what I have written is in the interest of giving a true picture of regular Army life in the twenties and thirties and is not intended to cause embarrassment to anyone.

In presenting life as I knew it at Jefferson Barracks, I have tried to tell the truth and in most cases have relied solely on my memory. But in reviewing these years I have been fortunate in finding family members and friends who have been willing to reinforce my memories with their own. I am particularly indebted to my mother who, although she did not always approve of what I said, was happy to have me say it, and to my childhood and college friends, Inett Layton Mueller and Henry Mueller, Cecile Grimble Arras, Vera Atkinson Baehr, Susan Ross Chambers, Frances Choate Kenner, and Clark Mills McBurney. Lt. Col. Sheldon Kirsner also helped with his recollections of Jefferson Barracks, as did Marion Bell and

221

Helen Bell Bonnot. My friend Clyde Maynard, who served in the Sixth Infantry Band with my father, gave me a full account of his recollections. Lt. Gen. Oren E. Hurlbut, who was my scoutmaster at Jefferson Barracks as a second lieutenant, has helped in invaluable ways. Mrs. Ethel Konzelman, who is responsible for the fine exhibits at the Jefferson Barracks Museum and for the restoration of the Laborer's House, gave me valuable advice over a long period of time and allowed me to use her unpublished *History of Jefferson Barracks*, drawn from various sources. Tony Fusco, who has devoted many years to the history of Jefferson Barracks, also gave me important pointers, and I have relied on his *A Pictorial History of Jefferson Barracks*, St. Louis, 1969. My greatest debt is to Sgt. William F. Alden, who also served in the Sixth Infantry Band with my father and knew him well. As historian of the Sixth Infantry, he has spent many hours with me going over events that we witnessed together and has allowed me to quote from his books, which I list below, and from the material that he has assembled on the subject of Jefferson Barracks. Mrs. Velma Gholson, the widow of Sergeant Gholson of B Company, was also helpful. My cousins Norman Smith, Verla Owen, Winton and Gladys Daniels, and my aunt Artelia Vought have aided with family materials in Arkansas, Louisiana, and Oklahoma.

My wife Sonja Haussmann Smith and my friends Helen Handley and Hannah Green were the first to read my finished text. Whatever grace it possesses owes much to these three graces. Lt. Col. H.F. Lippincott and Jack H. Mooney also read the finished text, and I am indebted to them both, and to Richard Wilbur for his suggestions. I am especially grateful to Holly Hall, Chief, Rare Books and Special Collections, Washington University Libraries, for her help in every phase of my investigation.

The records of many of the organizations that were once associated with Jefferson Barracks left with them and are scattered throughout the country. Many others disappeared when the post was deactivated. A brief history compiled by Capt. Harry E. Mitchell in 1921 was enlarged by Chaplain Walter B. Zimmerman and later by the Works Progress Administration in 1942. These histories were combined and enlarged in *The Story of Jefferson Barracks* by Maj. Henry W. Webb in 1944. This material was gathered together and supplemented in *Jefferson Barracks and the Sixth Infantry* by Ruth Layton and Alfred Bromet with William F. Alden, published by Layton, Layton & Associates, St. Louis, for the Sixth Infantry Association in 1961. In addition to these sources I am indebted to the following books and articles: William F. Alden, *It Happened in Lemay*, St. Louis, 1957; George Catlin, *Illustrations of the Manners, Customs, and Condition of the North American Indians with Letters and Notes*, 2 vols., London, 1866; C.W. Ceram, *The First American, A Story of North American Archaeology*, New York, 1971; Philip St. George Cooke, *Scenes and Adventures in the Army*, St. Louis, 1839; Angie Debo, *The Rise and Fall of the Choctaw Republic*, Norman, 1934; Samuel G. Drake, *Biography and History of the Indians of North America, from its first discovery*, Boston, 1841; Col. R. Ernest Dupuy, *The Compact History of the United States Army* (second revised edition), New York, 1973; *Encyclopedia of the History of Missouri*, St. Louis, 1901; John Gould Fletcher, *Life Is My Song: The Autobiography of John Gould Fletcher*, New York, 1937; Jack Foner, *The United States Soldier Between Two Wars: Army Life and Reforms, 1865-1898*, New York, 1970; Grant Foreman, *Indian Removal,* Norman, 1956; Paul Fussell, *The Great War and Modern Memory,* New York, 1975; John Gall, *Systemantics: How Systems Work and Especially How They Fail,* New York, 1977; Morris Janowitz, *The Professional Soldier, A Social and Political Portrait,* Glencoe, Illinois, 1960; James Jones, *WWII,* New York, 1975; Samuel H. Lockett, *Louisiana As It Is: A Geographical and Topographical Description of the State,* edited and with an introduction by Lauren C. Post, Baton Rouge, 1969; John E. Pfeiffer, "Indian City on the Mississippi," Time-Life Nature, Science Annual, 1974; Francis Paul Prucha, *Army Life on the Western Frontier: Selections from the Official Reports Made between 1826 and 1845 by Colonel George Croghan,* Norman, 1958; Francis Paul Prucha, *Broadax and Bayonet, The Role of The United States Army in the Development of the Northwest 1815-1860,* The State Historical Society of Wisconsin, 1953; Francis Paul Prucha, *The Sword of The Republic, The United States Army on the Frontier 1783-1846,* New York, 1969; J. Thomas Scharf, *History of St. Louis and St. Louis County,* Philadelphia, 1883; Major Amos Stoddard, *Sketches, Historical and Descriptive of Louisiana,* Philadelphia, 1812, New York, 1973; Captain Albert Tracy, "Missouri in Crisis" (from his journal), *Missouri Historical Review of the State Historical Society,* October, 1956; January, 1957; April, 1957; Alfred de Vigny, *The Military Condition (Servitude et grandeur militaires),* translation and notes by Marguerite Barnett, introduced by John Cruickshank, London, 1964; Dixon Wecter, *When Johnny Comes Marching Home,* New York, 1944; T. Harry Willams, *Huey Long,* New York, 1969; Frank R.E. Woodward, *The Dogs of War,* St. Louis, 1890; George Woodward, "Regular," *The New Yorker,* August 5, 1944.

I have also consulted the articles by Harley B. Bozeman in the *Winn Parish Gazette* (Winnfield, Louisiana). There are numerous articles about Jefferson Barracks in newspapers and journals but most of them repeat the same information. I have referred usually to those in the St. Louis *Post-Dispatch* and the St. Louis *Globe-Democrat* for the period covered and to the St. Louis *County Journal*, March 10, 1976, for information on the parachute jump of Albert Berry.

I wish to thank also the Columbia University Libraries; the Library of Congress; the Fishburn Library, Hollins College; the Jefferson Barracks Museum; the Missouri Historical Society; the Civil and Military Divisions, the National Archives; the University of Oklahoma Library; the Oklahoma Historical Society; the Division of Costume, Smithsonian Institution; the Library of the Virginia Military Institute; the Frances E. Willard Memorial Library for Alcohol Research, Evanston, Illinois; and the Willard Library, Battle Creek, Michigan.

—WJS